The Myth of Education in America

The Myth of Education in America

Students Should Be Taught How to Think, Not What to Think

Richard Hammes

ROWMAN & LITTLEFIELD
Lanham • Boulder • New York • London

Published by Rowman & Littlefield
An imprint of The Rowman & Littlefield Publishing Group, Inc.
4501 Forbes Boulevard, Suite 200, Lanham, Maryland 20706
www.rowman.com

86-90 Paul Street, London EC2A 4NE, United Kingdom

Copyright © 2022 by Richard Hammes

All rights reserved. No part of this book may be reproduced in any form or by any electronic or mechanical means, including information storage and retrieval systems, without written permission from the publisher, except by a reviewer who may quote passages in a review.

British Library Cataloguing in Publication Information Available

Library of Congress Cataloging-in-Publication Data

Names: Hammes, Richard, 1941– author.
Title: The myth of education in America : students should be taught how to think, not what to think / Richard Hammes.
Description: Lanham : Rowman & Littlefield, [2022] | Includes bibliographical references. | Summary: "This book provides a practical and implementable foundation for critical thinking as a broad-based solution to solving the education crisis"—Provided by publisher.
Identifiers: LCCN 2022023328 (print) | LCCN 2022023329 (ebook) | ISBN 9781475867770 (cloth) | ISBN 9781475867787 (paperback) | ISBN 9781475867794 (epub)
Subjects: LCSH: Critical thinking—Study and teaching—United States. | Education—Aims and objectives—United States. | Educational change—United States.
Classification: LCC LB1590.3 .H363 2022 (print) | LCC LB1590.3 (ebook) | DDC 370.15/2—dc23/eng/20220712
LC record available at https://lccn.loc.gov/2022023328
LC ebook record available at https://lccn.loc.gov/2022023329

To Dr. Michael Hakeem,
Preeminent Educator

For
All Teachers for Their Dedication
to Make the World Better

Contents

Acknowledgments	ix
Introduction	xi
Chapter 1: Is This Education?	1
Chapter 2: A Closer Look at the Current Classroom	19
Chapter 3: Why Critical Thinking Is Essential	31
Chapter 4: Educational Transformation	41
Chapter 5: Teaching Students to Think: The Foundation	47
Chapter 6: Implementation of Critical Thinking: The Hammes Classroom Experience	59
Chapter 7: What Now?: Actions to Take	89
Chapter 8: Hope for the Future	103
Bibliography	109
About the Author	113

Acknowledgments

First and foremost, I must acknowledge the professor that most influenced my education and teaching endeavors. Dr. Michael Hakeem was for me an educational giant and epitomized the best in classroom teaching. I am most appreciative of those who read the manuscript and offered their comments and insights based on their careers and knowledge of education. School superintendents Dr. Richard Moniuszko and Dr. Patricia Montgomery, middle school principal Dr. Sarah Owen, parent Christi Blaskowski, and university professor Dr. Sarah Amick. Of course, my wife, Barbara Hammes, a retired assistant superintendent for a special education district, was always supportive and encouraging, reading the book, editing, and providing her insightful analysis and suggestions along the way.

Introduction

> Teaching is not a delivery system of knowledge, rather it should stimulate, provoke, mentor, engage and facilitate learning.
>
> —Sir Ken Robinson

This quote serves as the perfect statement for the content of this book. Formal education is not just passing information through teachers to students, but rather the opportunity to discuss and evaluate it.

For most people there are moments in life that are transformational. It may not seem so immediately, but as you reflect back, even if it is just a few years, you can identify moments that changed how you thought about things or the direction of your career. The origin of my transformation of what I expected from my classroom experience as a student and teacher began in a criminology class taught by Dr. Michael Hakeem at the University of Wisconsin my sophomore year. Like many students I could not identify a major that excited me. I originally entered as a math major, moved to accounting, then to political science, and to educational counseling. However, it was this class in sociology that moved me in a new direction. Not the course content, although of interest, but rather the professor and his educational focus.

I majored in sociology but learned so much more about education and how to think and analyze material that the learning was far broader than my major. That professor focused on critical thinking and analysis, and it flipped a switch for me that changed the course of my life as well as all educational and teaching endeavors going forward. That first class was in a large lecture hall with over three hundred students. By the third week (the last week one could drop a class without cost) there were less than one hundred. Clearly, the students that dropped were not able or willing to try something different. His style was a radical change from any other class I had taken at any level of my education. When students from his classes went to other sociology classes and asked questions, the professor would say, you've been in Hakeem's class haven't you? They knew his teaching method but did nothing different than they had done for years. Lecture, discussion, questions, test, and move on to the next content. A disappointment.

The conventional classroom was routine and lacked the stimulus of thinking for myself and determining the validity of everything I read and heard. Several years later when I started my part-time teaching career in community colleges I implemented the conventional process of assigning chapters, lecturing on related content, and having the standard testing process. I had jokes in the column because it is important to keep students amused and brought to the class materials I thought students would find interesting.

When prior to starting the second semester I realized I could not do this, I had to utilize the techniques and style of learning that sociology professor had used and had such a profound impact on me. I spent long hours converting and developing new materials that focused on critical thinking and analysis. I stopped lecturing and instead engaged students in the hard work of questioning and analyzing the textbook and allied material. I found it exhilarating and freeing from the ties of content teaching and testing. This book will provide teachers with a foundation to implement similar teaching methods. It will also provide ideas and techniques to engage students, parents, and employers in the process. The utilization of critical thinking and analysis is a lifelong journey, and everyone can be involved in the process.

Although education may be thought of as any situation where we learn something, formal education in a classroom should offer more than "we learn something." Unfortunately, the focus of education from preschool to postdoctoral is on memorizing "facts" and data. The notion being that just knowing things is the most critical component of education.

This book emphasizes that the most important component of formal education is "how you learn" not "what you learn." If students are taught how to learn, they will retain content, but it will be based on analysis not on memorizing textbooks or notes from the teacher. How do we develop in students an ability to assess information and determine the value of the content they read and hear? The classroom is typically a place where students come to read books of "facts," be lectured by teachers/experts about the facts, and then repeat what they learned on examinations. This is not learning; this is force-feeding information and expecting students to regurgitate it when asked. There is little thinking going on, no analysis, no understanding of why or how, just memorization and the ability of students to retain information without regard to its probability that it is not the only content on any subject matter.

Of course, we want students to retain information, but not before they have evaluated it and determined why it is important to retain. Retention of content will flow automatically by reading, analyzing, and thinking about the material. This is an active process rather than one that highlights the main points for tests and overlooks supportive information or material that differs from the content emphasized in any classroom. This book provides an assessment of the status of education in America and what needs to be done if we want to develop thoughtful citizens who can address issues with analytical tools and make judgments based on the value of the information provided.

The case is made for teaching methods of learning rather than focusing exclusively on content. Students will remember what is important, but they will do so with a better understanding of why something is correct or important rather than merely accepting the authorities' pronouncement that it is. Facts are readily retained. Determining why they are facts, what other options exist, acknowledging opposing views and encouraging analysis takes more time, but this should be the foundation of learning.

The techniques for implementing can readily be used beyond the classroom. Parents of school age children can encourage them to utilize critical thinking skills to evaluate social situations as well as academic. They can engage teachers to assist students to think critically. Teachers at all levels of education from first grade through postgraduate school certainly should be focusing on teaching their students to be critically evaluative and encouraging them to determine what they think makes sense. Business and industry should be incorporating critical analysis in the day-to-day work of employees. Productivity can be enhanced if employees are seeking different ways to do things and questioning why things are done in certain ways. Finally, critical thinking is necessary in everyday life. The ability to sort out differing opinions, determine accuracy of data, evaluate options are all of value to function as responsible citizens.

It is important to note that the book is not finger-pointing at any specific group or organization, but rather the entire educational system that has accepted content memorization as the way to "educate" students.

The system is self-perpetuating in that all components feed into one another, and it seems impossible to promote change. Parents want their children to get into the best colleges, so they want them to pass exams and excel in content. Teachers are under pressure to ensure students meet the expectations of their parents and school administrators. School leadership is under pressure from their boards to have students excel to warrant taxes and attract people to their communities. Colleges are pressured to graduate students that will be employable. These and other factors combine to cause the educational system to focus on content and memorization rather than how to think, analyze, and make decisions about information. This is a huge web of inter-related educational components which makes the potential for changing our educational processes difficult, but it must be done. It cannot be said often enough, the role of the educator is to teach students how to think, not what to think. If this is done students will retain content, but only after analysis and discussion.

The first chapter focuses on what education is in the United States and countering views on why this is not education at all but rather indoctrination of "facts" memorized for tests and soon forgotten or of little value.

The second chapter overviews the state of education as students move through it from elementary school to postgraduate studies and how each step in the process further compounds the problem and makes it difficult to develop critical thinking in students.

The third chapter provides a review of why critical thinking should be more widely introduced and general suggestions on what to do to implement it in every classroom.

The fourth chapter provides insights into my educational transformation during my sophomore year in college and how it changed my life.

The fifth chapter is the foundation for critical thinking in the classroom. It provides the concepts for why it is necessary and the tools to implement critical thinking.

The sixth chapter overviews in detail what I did in my classes with examples, materials, and techniques to engage students in critical thinking. It illuminates how to open the minds of students to question everything and evaluate material regardless of the credentials of the source. There is a summation of the class, reflections on the future for the students, and my personal thoughts and feelings as each semester ended.

The seventh chapter provides detailed suggestions and encouragement for everyone to utilize critical thinking concepts, including parents, teachers, employers, and everyone in their daily life activities. This is not only an academic process, but also a tool for lifelong analysis of information, problem solving, and decision making.

The eighth chapter offers thoughts on the hope for the future regarding the potential for developing critical thinking as a core piece of the educational process.

The audience for this book is broad and encompasses all areas of our educational structure and society. It begins in the classroom, where the foundation for critical thought should be nourished and expanded. However, parents, employers, and others should be involved since critical thinking impacts all areas of our lives. I emphasize the classroom, but the real impact is the utilization of critical thinking regardless of our role and activity. Bringing critical thinking into the world of today is essential given the plethora of conflicting information we are bombarded with daily.

Everyone talks about the need to have parents, teachers, and others collectively involved in the educational work of students, but how does that occur?

Most parents have difficulty working with their children on the vast expanse of content. However, everyone can understand how to think critically, ask questions, wonder about alternatives, and not rely on one source for information. If we want parents involved, this is clearly a way for them to participate from pre-school until they graduate from high school. In this book parents will find useful ways to assist their children to be critical thinkers and perhaps gain insights themselves. The book is principally for educators and mainly at the college level, but critical thinking and analysis must begin much earlier and elementary, secondary, and high school teachers will find that this book is a guide for them as well. Teachers, students, and parents can utilize the ideas in this book to provide an integrated process for learning in and outside of the classroom.

We think of ourselves as the exceptional country, but we are slowly losing that status and much of that slide can be traced to our inability to effectively evaluate information and to seek alternatives to what we think and believe. If we do not equip students to do this, we have failed.

This book is a step forward in understanding the issues, gaining insights to basic techniques for critical thinking, and how to utilize logical principles and analytical tools to make the best judgments.

I will note several times in the book that obviously students (all of us) will accept a body of content that has a high probability of being correct and/or agreed upon. The point is to not accept it without viewing it with some critical analysis even though this will be more limited than for information that has clearly differing perspectives. Critically evaluating information is a process that promotes learning and retention. If you do this, what you need or want to remember will stick with you, but you will be more confident of its validity and value.

I know as teachers read further in this book, some may think, "But this will require us to revamp how we measure student progress." Yes, it will, and this will require some adjustment time. Content retention can still be evaluated, but it will be formatted in a way that requires students to think and evaluate it, not just recall it in some brief moment in time for a test. Rote memorization with no context or understanding is not education. Assessing how students determine the value of competing ideas or analyze and critique content is a far better "education."

As you venture into this book an impactful thought for readers is this: *Far more important than knowledge is the method by which it is reached.* Our educational system pounds "facts" into students with little time used to discuss the probability that there are other "facts" or, minimally, that these facts should be examined not merely memorized. Retained knowledge should be based on analysis and that is why critical thinking must be part of every course of study.

My classroom focused on being collaborative not competitive. Students exchanged research they had found, discussed differences, and determined what made the most sense to them as a group. There were no lectures. I provided information, but only to broaden the discussion and to add to what they researched and knew. The teacher is a guide not the sole determinant of what students should read and accept. Learning should not be competitive; it should be an opportunity to interchange and learn together. That is the basis of critical thinking and analysis. It removes competitive pressure and allows all students to participate and engage in discussions and learning experiences that are different from the norm.

Chapter 1

Is This Education?

> The object of education is to prepare the young to educate themselves throughout their lives.
>
> —Robert Hutch, Escotet Foundation

The quote opening this chapter should cause teachers to evaluate the teaching techniques they use in their classrooms. Are students being prepared with the tools and techniques necessary to be lifelong learners or is the focus on memorization of a limited body of content? Preparation for learning beyond the classroom requires learning techniques to sift through the plethora of information available and make judgments regarding its validity and utility. This chapter overviews the state of education during recent decades and how little it has changed during the past century.

Over the last several decades, the concept of education has broadened to include any life experience as well as any structured process to learn new information. In this sense, life is one extended educational process. Certainly, one can learn facts or opinions in a variety of ways, but is this education in the formal sense of evaluative learning and understanding? Is what is learned more important than how it is learned? Currently, formal education is a process wherein students get to know something based on the teacher telling them or reading a textbook and then being tested to ensure they retained the information. The system excels at this form of teaching, but it does so at the expense of critical thinking wherein learning is focused on analysis and collaborative thinking and discussion.

Although defining education in the context of the formal classroom may seem narrow, what the student takes to the world from this experience certainly broadens the impact. Therefore, the importance of the process of how and what students are taught is critical to how they will function beyond the classroom. If educators do not teach students how to question and analyze, they are merely developing memorizers and citizens that are not sufficiently able to make judgments based on sorting through options and evaluating information. At any given period in the history of this country, one can see that citizens not equipped to analyze what is happening often follow leaders or make decisions that are faulty and ill advised. Equipping them with the tools to make better choices will reduce the potential for making wrong decisions based on questionable information.

Defining what the educational process is currently and has been for a long time compared to what it should be is bolstered by the views of leading educational experts. Throughout this book the reader will find references to numerous educational leaders over the past hundred plus years. The scope of time is broadened to indicate that these perspectives on education are not new. Their thoughts are used to highlight issues and more importantly what they think should be the role of the teacher in the classroom.

Of course, the idea of thinking critically and asking questions is much older than the beginning of the twentieth century. Socrates in the fourth century BC was perhaps the originator. The Socratic Method postulates a give and take exchange among students and teachers, questioning everything.[1]

For the most part teaching of higher order thinking skills has not progressed much since Socrates postulated his principles of learning. The current educational system is quite the opposite focusing on memorization of "facts" with only superficial questioning and most of that focused on clarification rather than analysis.

Hutchins[2] states it succinctly when he asks if the university is to become an institution which attempts to indoctrinate its captives (students) to common opinion. The focus on action and practical application of knowledge has led to the classroom functioning merely as a purveyor of information needed to get a job or move on to the next higher-level course. A degree is the accumulation of information without regard to whether the knowledge gained is arguable and open to change, or merely information from a series of books and teachers that provided a very limited glimpse to what is available. The schools and the limited number of teachers students come in contact with determine what information their students will receive and what they think should be memorized.

Obviously, there is a need to gain knowledge as students proceed through the formal education years and there is some basic information everyone needs as a foundation. Everyone needs to learn an alphabet, numbers, reading, and other pieces of information that make it possible to function in the world. Within all fields of study there are some foundational pieces of information that allow students to build their knowledge base and explore the breadth of content available. In practitioner fields such as medicine, accounting, and teaching, there is basic information to understand the rudiments necessary to begin working. However, beyond the basics the expanse of information, techniques, and possibilities provides an enormous array of differences that need exploration without influence from the teacher pushing students in one direction or another.

Teachers should certainly offer what they know, and students should have textbooks as a starting point, but the classroom experience should be bigger than this and provide students with guidance to do research, to read differently, to evaluate content, and generally expose them to the enormous content available without prejudice toward one set of "facts" or biased views of what is best.

It is likely that no teacher at any grade level from elementary through postgraduate school has more than 5 percent of the knowledge and information available in their areas of "expertise." They typically have a textbook, some additional resource material, and likely some additional knowledge, but this does not scratch the surface of the information available. How can students be certain that the teacher's 5 percent is better or more accurate than someone else's 5 percent? They can't. But this is not questioned but rather everyone just takes it at face value that what students are taught in any classroom is the best information available and constitutes the information everyone needs in any given subject. This is not what education should be especially in the twenty-first century. It can and must be better in order to prepare students to meet the challenges of the information age. Everyone is overwhelmed with information with limited ability to assess it. This will be personalized further in the book.

Compounding the problem, many teachers feel an obligation to take positions on social issues in order to appear relevant, but this is not their role. Rather than influencing students they should be assisting them to sort through differences and give them the tools and encouragement to gather information on all sides of an issue and then guide them through analysis to form their own judgments.

This naturally segues into a critical concern that has arisen since the 1990s. With the advent of various social media options, the plethora of misinformation is overwhelming and seemingly accepted by many regardless of the source or any supportive evidence. There is limited personal ability to sort through fact from fiction or minimally what may have supportive evidence versus outright intentional lies to foment anger and disrupt social discourse.

Despite some progress in teaching critical-thinking skills, most employers state that employees lack the ability to think critically and solve problems. They require clear direction and will seek guidance rather than attempt to work through a problem. Arum and Roksa[3] caused a stir when the authors asserted that students made little to no progress in critical-thinking ability during their college years, mainly because little effort was made to encourage it. With all of the issues we confront daily, it is paramount to develop critical-thinking skills in citizens to give them the potential to sort through the misinformation and appeals to emotion. Teachers must teach students how to think.

As an adjunct professor at several community colleges in the metropolitan Chicago area for more than forty years, the author taught a range of psychology courses, principally introductory. Every semester began with two questions for students. What is the purpose of education and why are they here in this class and in college? As one might expect these questions garnered similar responses semester after semester.

Consistently, students noted that the purpose of education was to learn things, help to get a better job, broaden knowledge base, make more money, and similar objectives. Most were in this class because it was a social science requirement, seemed like it could be interesting, needed a few more credits for a degree, and similar things.

These discussions would take some time and not once in all of those years did a student mention learning how to think critically or as we emphasized just now how to think. After writing their thoughts on the board a discussion would follow about each thought. After this discussion one idea was written on the white board as the purpose of formal education and that is to think.

This was expanded upon by saying that students think they know how to think but no one has taught them how to think, so it is unlikely they can think in the sense students will learn in this class. Students will learn about psychology, receive and read content, but it will be done differently, and they will leave the class much different than when they arrived.

This is the purpose of formal education, to inculcate in students the ability to think, which means analyze information and determine what makes sense to them based on using logical principles and other analytical tools. If teachers fail to do this, they have not educated students, they have merely jammed information into them that they then repeat on tests, will soon forget most of what they learned, and are not sure what to do with what they have retained.

The role of the instructor is not to push information but to offer an environment in which the students are taught how to critically evaluate information, compare it to other information, and make decisions regarding what they think makes sense to them. What are thought to be facts today may not be facts tomorrow. This includes any course of study. There is essentially nothing that is absolute fact. Everything is a probability, some more highly probable than others, but nothing is absolute.

Of course, this mystified most students in the class and when the class period ended the last statement to the students was the hope that most of them would return next week, knowing that some students cannot deal with ambiguity and change and therefore would not return. They want "facts" and the comfort of making check marks on a page to questions to pass tests and move on to the next class. That is education to them. However, for those that did return (most) the experience was like no other they had or likely would have in future classes.

But why do some students not return? It likely is because they are comfortable with the routine of the typical classroom in America, wherein a textbook is provided, and lectures of allied material are given. Teachers walk them through the book. Have some occasional discussion. Provide periodic tests that force them to memorize the limited information they receive. There is little ambiguity, no reason to question the information provided, and it is a process they know and have adapted to.

Thinking causes pain and like good utilitarians students will do whatever they can to avoid pain. Just tell them what they need to know, test them to make sure they know it, and then let's move on to the next isolated segment of information. Why should they evaluate what is written in a textbook or provided by the instructor? Both have done research and are providing what they think is important for students to know. That is good enough.

That is the predominant education schema in America, and it is part of the reason over the past several decades the United States has moved in the wrong direction compared to numerous other countries. America is losing its dominance in terms of being the most innovative, most analytical, and most productive nation. Employees, like students, after years of being directed on what and how to learn also want clear direction in the workplace. They want no ambiguity, and they have limited desire to analyze. They want to do the job as prescribed and go home because that is how they are taught from an early age, and they are used to that routine.

This needs to change if the country is to enhance the potential for growth. In particular, the university should be a center of independent thought, although education at every level should encourage this.

Many students (and teachers) will note that this may work in the social sciences or for any field of study that has an inexactitude, but not for sciences and mathematics which have solid evidence for their conclusions.

This perspective is not correct; nearly everything can and should be debatable at some level. Certainly, there are "facts" in every field of study that one could posit are not worth debating since the probabilities they are correct are extremely high, but this does not negate that a large proportion of "facts" are not highly probable and should be open to critical evaluation. Obviously, the social sciences have fewer near absolutes than the physical sciences and that is why this focus in psychology classes tends to more readily engage students. However, this does not negate the fact that critical thinking is of value in all fields of study.

There are many points postulated by those who think teachers should not emphasize critical thinking. Here are several offered by Hook[4] among other contrarians.

1. Focusing on critical evaluation creates a mood of skepticism, exaggerated distrust, and cynical debunking.
2. It is incompatible with action which our society needs to promote change. It makes us tentative when we should be decisive.
3. It spells the death of vision. It may inspire a passion for clarity, but it is the shining clarity of empty glasses.
4. Truth has many mansions which are not accessible to scientific method and analysis and the latter becomes a cult rather than enlightenment.
5. We are bound up in minutia which reduces productivity.

Of course, there are more that could be listed, but let's address these since they are certainly a core of the concerns. Those who support some or all of the five points above would retort that doing this will use some of the same critical techniques they say are not always useful or of value.

The first point is correct, but not in the negative way it portrays. The process of critical thinking and scientific method is to promote skepticism, distrust, and debunking, because much of what is promoted as fact deserves this framing. Even if something has some factual basis, if there are other possibilities, then we should be skeptical and distrusting, although not necessarily outright debunking. However, critical thinking does not automatically call for throwing out the baby with the bath. Rather, nearly everything is debatable and deserves scrutiny. Although many things may be highly probable, there often are optional views equally well-documented that call the "fact" into question. This is what education and learning should be, a continual debate, push and pull of differing opinions, theories, and facts with differing foundations. Just memorizing what one book or one teacher says are the facts is not education and everyone should be skeptical, distrusting and debunking of educators and schools that think this is fine.

The second point raises a critical concern with our society in general, that action and activity are more essential than thinking and analyzing. The athlete is cherished as action oriented, and the professor denigrated as passive. One brings the thrill of victory, the other lives in an ivory tower with their head in the clouds. For example, a child from age five to age sixteen practices ice skating several hours every day and ends by going to the Olympics and most worship this by saying how dedicated and focused the person was to achieve so much. Another child within the same age span goes to the library and spends time reading and excelling in school and most say what a nerd, the child should get a life. To a large degree Americans are anti-intellectual which is further supported by the obscene incomes of athletes, versus those of professors and teachers in general. Who is providing more to advance society? That should not be a question since it is self-evident.

The classroom is not the place for action, it is the one environment (or one of very few) that should promote analytical thinking. There is no pressure to reach a decision only to explore the wide range of information available on any topic or issue. Transferring this to the work world, yes action must be taken, but too often actions occur without proper analysis and without critically evaluating an action before going forward. Yes, decisions need to be made, but wouldn't it be better to do so after taking time to be evaluative of the actions about to be undertaken? Shouldn't options be sought, comparisons made, potential outcomes determined before decisions are made? Even when time is limited, making an effort to analyze a decision or action before implementing it seems logical and prudent. Formal education, and particularly the university, should not be focused on decision making. It should be focused on deliberation and analysis. When it moves to be involved in deciding what is best or not it no longer is an educational institution, but an institution that is just another arm of business, politics, or other organizations that must make decisions. There should be at least one place where making decisions is not the main importance, even though students will make decisions based on their own analysis.

The third concern is cute in the sense of being visually cutting, but is vision really curtailed because it might be of value to step back and determine whether or not someone is seeing clearly or just reacting to something that fits their thinking and knowledge base? Is it the "death" of vision? Is it better to venture forward without analyzing hazards because it is thought to be visionary? Making the wrong determination causes more delay in getting to the right conclusion because one must go back and start again. Better an empty glass than one filled with something that may be harmful or just wrong. As a self-proclaimed actionist, sometimes taking time to explore options or minimally, the pros and cons of acting seems prudent even for someone that prefers action over too much deliberation.

Again, in academic settings everything needs evaluation, not to curtail visionaries, but to assess pros and cons of any idea or action. That is the main function of the classroom to encourage students to think. If teachers provide the tools to think and evaluate critically, their visionary thrusts are far more likely to lead in a sound direction. Of course, visionaries and actionists are needed, but we need the pragmatists and evaluators as well. If teachers can equip students to understand both sides, the world will be far better off.

The fourth point alludes to a notion that there are some things that are not accessible by scientific method or critical thinking. What truth cannot be evaluated? What truth is not open to discussion or variant points of view?

Accepting certain things as truths does not mean there cannot be any possibility of an alternative perspective.

Russell[5] contends that if the experts are agreed, then the opposite position cannot be held to be certain. If the experts are not agreed, then no position can be held to be certain. This should be a placard in every classroom because it emphasizes the point that essentially nothing is absolute. Again, it is acknowledged that some facts are highly probable and unlikely to be contested, but that is a comparatively minute amount of information in any field. Nearly universally, for most things, the experts are not agreed. For those select things wherein they are agreed, the opposite position could still be correct since everything is a probability.

There may not be different sets of facts, but there may be variances in how one can logically view something and how it compares to other alternatives. There must be verifiability instead of the loose notion that truths have many mansions and therefore are not open to thinking about them.

The fifth point speaks to the anti-intellectual who wants simplified thinking, easy answers to complex questions, and values action over thinking. It may be minutia, but often the real answer is in the tightly wound inner core of an issue that takes time to unravel. Can productivity be enhanced by ensuring the right decisions are being made based on analysis and discovery? Starting in the wrong direction and needing to go back is a waste of time as well as limiting the potential success of an endeavor.

There are likely other points of opposition to critical thinking and scientific method, but these five are an amalgamation of the usual negative views of "over-using these techniques." The point should be, is it better to overthink something and move in the right direction or not critically assess an action or thought and potentially move in the wrong direction. None of these points seem scholarly and certainly do not describe what an academic setting should promote. In the world outside of academia there are times when swift decision making is needed, but even then, a little time should be taken to determine potential negative outcomes or how the decision could be improved.

If experts, scholars, teachers, and other academicians think that teaching facts and focusing on content is the only way to impart knowledge then we are in the decline of thinking and are moving in the direction of computers, which only function based on the data pushed into them. Computers do not have the ability to abstract something or to think about it differently than the information put into them (although there are some computers now that have some limited ability to process information in differing ways and this may be even more likely in the future). Humans can take information, incorporate it with other information, dissect it, repackage it, and ultimately determine the value or lack of value for any piece of information. Why not use this ability and encourage and grow it?

The role of a teacher is to encourage thinking. To debate differing views, to not accept something merely because an expert or many experts have determined an answer (or it is in a textbook or some website). It is the teacher's responsibility to give students the tools to evaluate information, look for alternatives, and determine for themselves what they think is the "right" answer. Students do not come armed with these tools. Obviously, there are some teachers doing this, but the educational system makes it difficult.

Expanding more on why some think critical thinking is a drag on creativity and innovation, what does that mean exactly? Creativity is not solely the province of those who lack a critical mind or those who react quickly and make quick decisions. Indeed, critical thinking is a significant component of creative thought. It is the ability to step back and look at something or evaluate a train of thought that promotes creative thinking. Creative thinkers look at things and wonder how they could be different or ask why we do what we do. It is their ability to be critically evaluative that spurs new ideas, concepts, or widgets.

In this century people are overwhelmed with information and "facts." Clearly, followers of certain news outlets or leaders often receive a very biased view of the world, specific issues, and are brainwashed to "believe" not think. They have an emotional connection, not one based on evaluation and an objective perspective. Toffler[6] in the 1970s spoke of the time that was coming in the near future when people would be overwhelmed by information and unable to keep up or sort through it all. Toffler foresaw mental processing issues, a sense of being crushed by information and potentially incapacitated. Indeed, that state has existed for more than twenty years.

It has been labeled the information age but being overloaded with information and misinformation requires the ability to sort through it to make logical choices. We need to build up our ability to process and sort through information in order to reduce the impact of too much information which is confusing, contradictory, and sometimes just wrong.

Just having some basic logical reasoning concepts and techniques to evaluate what one reads and hears will greatly assist filtering information and making choices. This cannot be accomplished by focusing on memorization, rarely questioning information, and not seeking alternatives. The educational system is setting up students to fail in the sense that they are not equipped to meet the challenges of the information age.

Hutchins[7] states, "The best definition of a university that I have been able to think of is that it is a center of independent thought. It may be a good many other things as well; but if it is not this, it has failed. The principal function of a professional school in a university is not to train people for the profession, but to criticize the profession." It is thoughts such as these that caused some to question Hutchins' educational philosophy, but Hutchins as chancellor of the University of Chicago for more than twenty years strengthened that university as one of the best in the world. Certainly, professional schools must prepare students for their profession, but if they are not taught to be critical of it and question that content, who will? Who is more qualified than those in a profession to criticize it because they know more than those not in it?

However, our professional schools are for the most part not academic in the sense of encouraging assessment, critical evaluation, and discourse that creates change. Instead, they are merely training schools, pumping "facts" into students, and churning them through the system and out to the work world with limited ability to self-evaluate or look beyond the "facts" they have learned. Here and there a student might venture beyond and maybe even become more analytical after graduating. Why not help them along the way by providing the tools and skills to be critical thinkers?

This becomes self-evident in the field of psychology when one looks at various schools of thought. The content (bias) the student has regarding psychological theories, treatment techniques, and research is for the most part based on the school attended and/or the teacher. Various major universities emphasize specific schools of thought and train their students with this focus. Therefore, depending upon the school students graduated from they might be a Behaviorist, Gestalt, Humanist, Psychoanalytic, or some other narrow theory based on the work of those who espouse them and the teachers that promote them. Students might get a smattering of other content, but if they want to be a clinician, they focus on one and become an "expert." This is not education, and it certainly does not produce graduates with a broad base of knowledge, nor the ability to evaluate the pros and cons of a range of theories and decide for themselves what makes sense, which might be an amalgamation of theories rather than one.

However, we are becoming increasingly more concerned with training experts to fill specified positions and therefore cramming them with information deemed important to function in a role. The more technologically advanced the world becomes the more there is a need for trained specialists, and this is usually the first reason advanced for training rather than education. But it is more than this, it is the widespread degradation of education in this country and a general dislike for the intellectual and academician. Political push over the past several decades clearly indicates that action and narrow thinking are desired by a sizable portion of citizens. They do not want to hear contrary opinions and are convinced the other side wants to destroy the country and negatively impact their lives. There is no give and take, no exploration of opposing views, and no desire to seek agreement.

The role of the professor is viewed as a professional teaching the apprentices for a specific job in the field. Rather than expanding the knowledge base, this teaching process is focused on ensuring the student memorizes specific content the teacher thinks is important to perform a task, with little regard for the likelihood that what is fact today may not be in the future. Or minimally, it will be modified and not be the same fact.

Just how expert are the "experts"? How much knowledge of an entire field of study can any one person retain? As a teacher the statement to the class suggested that it is not possible to know more than a small percentage of the total knowledge available. Honestly it is not possible to answer every question students may have with the breadth it deserves. It is improbable that any teacher or professional can, although many teachers may respond as though they do have all of the answers. There are hundreds of research studies and articles written every month, hundreds of books published and, of course, there is the internet overflowing with information, likely less reliable in many instances, but available. It is not possible to access but a small percentage of this information. Therefore, teachers rely on a textbook author to do the research, but even then, how much can they put into one book surveying the field? It is an impossible task, but teachers rely on the textbook writer anyway to provide them with the "key" information for each course, without thinking about the personal bias of the authors regarding what they research and what they think is most important to know. Or, even worse what they think are the "facts" while ignoring other counter perspectives or facts.

Certainly, it is necessary to start with some content to impart some reasonably prevailing knowledge in a field of study. However, it is the role of the teacher to guide students through these books and assist them to evaluate the information, seek additional resources, and not rely on them as the only information available regardless of the supposed validity. If teachers remind themselves that authors cannot cover the wide expanse of knowledge available, they will understand the value of questioning what textbooks offer and raise questions about the content provided.

What is the fear of critical thought? Why do proponents of particular viewpoints condemn criticism and possible alternatives? Perhaps it is related to Hutchins'[8] point concerning the position of a political system (i.e., country) toward critical thought. He states that totalitarian countries (and likely many democracies as well) do not encourage people to exercise critical judgment. Hutchins further postulates that such countries may produce experts of every kind, including experts in indoctrination, and institutions of "higher learning" are really dedicated to training not education.

Based on attitudes toward professors, especially in Ivy League schools, America is an anti-intellectual society. Large portions of the population scorn those in their ivory towers or with their head in the clouds. They want a focus on training people for specialized fields and this causes educators and schools to continually narrow the scope of what students learn in the classroom.

In Western cultures intelligence is viewed as a means for individuals to devise categories and to engage in rational debate. In Eastern cultures, it is viewed as a way for members of a community to recognize contradiction and complexity and play their social roles effectively. This does not mean that everyone shares the culture's style of thinking, but it is an overarching process and value.[9] This provides a basis for why different cultures approach education and learning differently and also why their analytical skills vary.

This can be moved deeper into Western culture particularly in America, wherein knowledge is prized and many are annoyed by those who raise questions or challenge traditional thought. We want answers not explanations. The teacher that is most lauded is the one who has students that perform well on tests. Teachers are trapped in a world that demands class ranks and the ability of students to score well on college entrance exams. There are many "high performing" schools in this country that focus their curriculum and teaching structure to ensure their students can pass standardized tests and will therefore get into the best universities. There is limited concern for what the information means or searching for alternative answers. Parents in these districts have moved there because it will help their children in college selection. This is not education nor learning of the highest order. This is merely learning efficiency. Its aim is to maximize the amount of information acquired per unit of time. The image is one of students, like geese, being force-fed as much educational nourishment they can take without retching. Often another outcome is students become averse to learning other than in doses of information they can use to achieve a short-term goal. They have no love of some of the joys of learning, which include the interchange of ideas, analysis of personal thinking on a topic, and reaching conclusions based on personal analysis and effort.

What educational institutions are doing instead at all levels is rewarding diligence, persistence, and content retention, not the ability to analyze and think. If students pore over details for hours a day, these students likely will do well on benchmark tests, but do these students really understand the material if there is no analysis or effort to integrate it with other information? Most people have a broad range of information stored, but likely don't understand it with any depth. It is merely "facts" that come to the surface when needed, even though they may not be the only facts available or even correct.

When teaching, students are asked why it is important to memorize dates and events. Most often the response is to pass tests. For the most part just reading about them most will stick with us without multiple reviews to ensure they are remembered for a test. For instance, the date 1066 is readily recalled by the author (even though it is not of any apparent value to remember this date). Asking students what is significant about that date universally brought blank stares, except one semester a student from England knew it was the Battle of Hastings. The point is what is the value of knowing that date? It did not mean anything, but it was recalled because it was stored in memory without intense memorization. Good for a trivia game, but otherwise? Wouldn't it be better to know why that battle was important and what consequence it brought? Even more focused, are there different perspectives regarding why this battle was important and what outcomes came from it?

Memorization of dates and events or theories and formulas have little value if we do not push students to analyze the information and determine why it is important and what other information might be of value. Otherwise, such detail is easily retrievable. Most information people retain has not been memorized for a test, but rather retained in the course of reading or hearing about it. However, the skills and techniques to analyze it are not readily gained without initial guidance.

Students seeking to exercise their brains and explore material in more depth and expanse are bored by the routine of the educational model which begins in first grade and never changes throughout the long educational process. Whitehead[10] noted that schooling in the United States is a mile wide and an inch deep. Fragmentary topics are taught, quickly memorized, tested, and then forgotten. In the history of education, the most striking phenomenon is that schools of learning exhibit routine. They are dull and lack challenge for students because they are overladen with inert ideas and this education is not only useless, but harmful.

Similarly, Barzun[11] states that people with doctoral degrees will remember later in life that there were two weeks in preparation for final exams when they knew everything, now it is gone.

The Library of Congress[12] found that 40 percent of seventeen-year-old students could not draw inferences from written material and only 20 percent could write a persuasive essay. Given the state of education today even more focused on testing, these numbers are likely going to get worse.

A significant issue with our educational process is the focus and reliance on multiple choice questions to indicate how much a student has retained. Nothing promotes learning less than making check marks on a sheet of paper and being satisfied with the retention of memorized material. Standardized tests trivialize learning and give a distorted picture of a student's intellectual skills.[13] Students take these tests and quickly forget most of what they memorized. It has no value to them and nothing to tie it together to promote retention. It is just an isolated piece of information without regard for the integration and expansion of it in an analytical manner.

Pushing through content without thought has little value. Students need time to ponder and evaluate content.[14]

Essentially this is contrasting teaching as content versus method. "Far more important than knowledge is the method by which it is reached, and the ability to recognize when it constitutes evidence and when not; and more important than any particular ideal is the way in which it is held, and the capacity to evaluate it in relation to other ideals. . . . Our educational institutions especially on the college level, must emphasize method of analysis."[15] Most educators would give passing acknowledgment that this is correct, but when teachers walk into the classroom, they continue to emphasize content lectures with limited effort to evaluate the material presented. The University of Wisconsin has as its guiding educational philosophy posted on the door of the main education building, "Whatever may be the limitations which trammel inquiry elsewhere, we believe that the great state University of Wisconsin should ever encourage that continual and fearless sifting and winnowing by which alone the truth can be found." This does not mean pounding a narrow range of information but rather opening up the field of study to engage in discourse, weighing pros and cons and reaching conclusions only after an exhausting review and analysis. This is education as it should be. They wrote this in 1894. What has happened to that perspective over the last century and more?

The professor that influenced the author the most viewed the state of education as intellectual robbery in that it is stealing minds and preventing students from thinking on their own and developing an analytical mind. The educational system takes over the students' ability to process information and overpowers them with a small cadre of facts. Much like actual robbery, students are forced to accept what the system contends their brains should contain and not allow for thinking, analysis, and freedom of decision making. What can be more debilitating than that? For the most part the educational system K–12 limits what teachers can do. At the college level there is more freedom, but departments regulate and guide textbook selection and overall course content.

In all of the courses this professor taught, he never used a textbook. Instead, there were selections reproduced from a wide range of resources, providing conflicting perspectives and questioning of the mainstream thinking in the field. Textbooks offer what one or several authors think is the essential information necessary based on the course description. Different textbooks provide different pieces of information, although much of it is the same. There is no significant effort to question the material. It is assumed that their summary of the basic information should be memorized and retained since it contains what they think is most important. This despite the obvious, which is most of it is not the absolute answer and even if highly probable, should still be analyzed and questioned. This is not to say that textbooks should not be used, although it is of concern, but rather the concern is with how they are used.

This professor never published a book and did not go on speaking engagements. His perspective was to be a dispassionate and objective teacher and therefore he would not indulge in these ego-building actions. He did publish a few articles critiquing information. If one believes that everything should be questioned and that no body of information is absolute, it is impossible to write a book about content in the field, unless it can be several thousand pages to allow for questioning and a range of views. This was the foundation for the author's approach to education and how students should learn.

However, textbooks are not the only concern (since they can be used differently), although a significant one. College teachers have relative freedom to develop their course presentations with little constraint, but it appears few are making a concerted effort to introduce critical thinking as a core feature of the classroom. This book should provide the impetus to try a different approach. It should energize teachers. They will find teaching much more challenging because focusing on critical thinking requires a revamping of course content and the ebb and flow of every class day will be different. These teachers are free to change how they conduct the classroom experience and what they provide for students. This book offers why and how to do it.

K–12 education is different in that there are some restrictions on what can be done in the classroom. Although these teachers are admittedly constrained by an accountability-based system where testing rules, they must be the leaders of change. It will not be easy, but who is better equipped to challenge the way teaching is conducted in the classroom than teachers? They should not concede their domain. Certainly, there are many teachers trying to change the educational process, but not in the way the author thinks is needed. Unfortunately, teaching using a textbook as the resource for lectures, preparing and presenting this content in a regimented manner, ensuring that all chapters are covered and key content is highlighted is a comfortable routine. This allows for limited time for questioning the material since all course content must be covered to prepare for tests. After years of indoctrination, teachers are not prepared to vary from the process they learned in schools of education, participated in for years, and is expected by the administration and parents. For the most part the student could do much of this on their own with some limited guidance. They do not need a teacher to help them read. Occasionally, teachers may offer some material outside of the textbook, but this is to bolster the information already provided. It is likely rare that teachers are providing contradictory material or anything that would question what exists in the textbook.

Even varying techniques to present material does not alter the fact that it remains indoctrination to the facts provided by teachers via the textbook or other material. It often is merely entertainment. The teacher is the resident expert, and the students are there to listen, take notes, ask for some clarification, and then take tests to ensure that the teacher will be viewed as imparting "knowledge." It is again emphasized that teachers are trapped by the expectations of parents, administrators, the community, local business owners and others to produce high test scores on standardized tests. It is difficult to introduce critical thinking in these circumstances.

Therefore, there is little or no effort to present opposing views, evaluate the information provided in terms of how conclusions are reached or requiring students to find varying material via library or internet research. Students are often reluctant to do this because they have been conditioned to not question whatever experts tell them, including the teacher. It is important to note that one need not be an expert to ask questions and ponder the validity or value of content read or presented. Otherwise, most of us could rarely question things we are not "expert" in. We must encourage questioning as an essential component of critical thinking.

Hullfish and Smith state "that to learn a method of thinking is of greater importance than to learn any specific set of facts. Indeed, the claim may be more strongly put . . . namely, apart from gaining control of the method of reflection it is impossible to LEARN any facts at all."[16] Therefore, memorization teaching should be reduced to some "basic content" to provide a foundation and then balanced with critical thinking and reflection. They add, "We may say that true education is concerned with the steady, unremitting, progressive development of intelligence as revealed through an increasing capacity and disposition on the part of each individual to think."[17] Knowledge without evaluation is an empty vessel and unfulfilling. To use a phrase regarding the content on television, "a vast wasteland."[18]

Based on a career as a clinical and then organizational psychologist, many of the comments and examples in this book will be based on these two careers and more generally the social sciences. However, this emphasis does not mean that the same focus should not be present in every field of study including mathematics, all sciences, medicine, history, and so forth. Every field has its "facts," and some are more probable than others, but there are vast areas of content that are open to critical assessment and multiple interpretations. Some less than others, but none exempt from critical thinking and opportunity for analysis to open the minds of students to potentially viable alternatives.

Some final thoughts on "is this education." Openness and free expression are benchmarks of the American culture, but it is often silenced from elementary through graduate school. You can have your thoughts and beliefs outside of the four walls of the classroom, but typically in the classroom the information flow is in one direction and discussion is only to clarify not question, expand, or discount. A University of Chicago president may have summed up university education best when asking, "Do you know what it means when you hand somebody a diploma. What are you certifying? Is it that they sat in classes for four years and passed some tests and wrote some papers?" The article goes on to say that it should not be, but rather it should be to learn to be open and deliberative, to judge ideas by their merits and wield sharp analytical tools across all areas of knowledge.[19]

This last citation sums up what this book proposes and what the reader will find as they read on and gain insights into specific concerns, what others propose the classroom should offer and implement, and what the author developed for implementation in the classroom during a lengthy teaching career.

NOTES

1. Plato, *Early Socratic Dialogues,* edited by Trevor J. Saunders (London: Penguin Classics, 2005), 85.

2. Robert Hutchins, *The University Utopia* (Chicago: University of Chicago Press, 1953), 123.

3. Richard Arum and Josipa Roksa, *Academically Adrift* (Chicago: University of Chicago Press, 2011), 32.

4. Sidney Hook, *Education for the Modern* (New York: The Dial Press, 1946), 109.

5. Howard Woodhouse, "The Concept of Growth in Bertrand Russell's Educational Thought," *Journal of Educational Thought* 17, no. 1 (1983): 47–61.

6. Alvin Toffler, *Future Shock* (New York: Penguin Random House, 1970), 43.

7. Robert Hutchins, "The Idea of a College," *The Center Magazine* 5, no. 3, 46.

8. Robert Hutchins, *The Conflict in Education in a Democratic Society* (New York: Harper and Bros., 1956), 185.

9. Richard Nisbett, *The Geography of Thought* (New York: Free Press, 2003), 66.

10. Alan Lesgold, "The Nature and Methods of Learning and Doing," *The American Psychologist* (November 2001): 24–33.

11. Jacques Barzun, *The House of Intellect* (New York: Harper Perennial, 2002), 184.

12. Library of Congress, Education Study, 1984.

13. Theodore Sizer, *Redesigning the American High School* (Boston: Houghton Mifflin, 1992), 54.

14. Suzanne Plaut, *The Right to Literacy in Secondary Schools: Creating a Culture of Thinking* (New York: Teachers College Press, 2012), 78.

15. Sidney Hook, *Education for the Modern* (New York: The Dial Press, 1946), 77.

16. H. Gordon Hullfish and Philip G. Smith, *Reflective Thinking: The Method of Education* (New York: Dodd, Mead and Co., 1968), 97.

17. Hullfish and Smith, *Reflective Thinking*, 102.

18. Newton H. Minnow, Chairman Federal Communications Commission, 1960 in a speech.

19. Lucas McGranahan, "Defining Figure," *The University of Chicago Magazine* (Spring 2021): 13.

Chapter 2

A Closer Look at the Current Classroom

Readers are plentiful. Thinkers are rare.

—Harriet Martineau

The quote to open this chapter is simple yet expansive. The educational system is proficient at teaching students how to read and retain small blocks of information but has not been as effective on developing thinking and analysis.

The first chapter provided an overview of some general concerns within our education system. This chapter highlights the spectrum of concerns as individuals advance through the education system, beginning in elementary school, through graduate school, and into adulthood, as well as the impacts on other aspects of our society. There are some countering suggestions offered that can expand and enhance the educational process at every grade level. More extensive implemental ideas are provided in chapter 7. The modern school is a hierarchical structure of authority in the "reproduction" of knowledge.[1] It relies on control and the absoluteness of what is being taught. Teaching focuses almost exclusively on content. Parents want their students to excel on standardized tests and get into the best possible colleges. Administrators and teachers often respond to this pressure to teach to the test and ensure students excel on fact-based benchmarks.

Since schools of education (i.e., teacher preparation programs) focus on content teaching, curriculum development, classroom management, and basic techniques of teaching, teachers have had minimal or no modeling of how to focus on critical thinking in the classroom.

Over the past sixty plus years, Bloom's taxonomy has been one of the foundational processes for classroom teaching. Although it is somewhat diminished in its influence, it continues to be cited as one of the key learning processes.

- Knowledge involves the recall of specifics and universals, the recall of methods and processes, or the recall of a pattern, structure, or setting.
- Comprehension refers to a type of understanding or apprehension such that the individual knows what is being communicated and can make use of the material or idea being communicated without necessarily relating it to other material or seeing its fullest implications.
- Application refers to the use of abstractions in particular and concrete situations.
- Analysis represents the breakdown of a communication into its constituent elements or parts such that the relative hierarchy of ideas is made clear and/or the relations between ideas expressed are made explicit.
- Synthesis involves the putting together of elements and parts to form a whole.
- Evaluation engenders judgments about the value of material and methods for given purposes.

Bloom's taxonomy is a pyramidal learning structure that has content memorization as the foundation of learning. It postulates that analysis and creative thinking come only after memorization, which is the overwhelming focus of this taxonomy.[2]

Although to a limited degree the taxonomy is correct, it fails to integrate critical thinking and creative analysis early in the process. Instead, the taxonomy treats these as add-ons to the learning process rather than an integral component from the outset of formal education. Emphasizing critical thinking in the classroom turns this upside down. Analysis and creative thinking are intertwined with content learning and are an essential part of the foundation.

When students arrive at college their prior twelve years of content memorization learning makes it a formidable task for college teachers to overcome. Given the structure of colleges and the importance placed on preparing students for careers it is difficult for teachers even at this level to deviate much from content memorization instruction. Some teachers may offer some critiques of information and perhaps provide countering views to the prevailing position, but this is limited by the need to ensure the required content is covered in a specified time period. It takes significant effort to overcome this focus on content memorization. This chapter provides an overview of how this content focused learning process is nurtured through the years of education.

Development of critical thinking and analysis is a gradual process of learning. Changing one's habits of thought is a long-range project, happening over years.[3] This is why teaching students to think critically should begin in their first years of formal classroom instruction and even earlier with parental involvement. Critical thinking lays the foundation for further intellectual development. It must begin early and be built upon until students become skilled at developing sophisticated arguments and responses to questions while encouraging them to determine the validity of premises and conclusions. Unfortunately, for the most part, our education system has failed.

THE EARLY YEARS: PRE-K TO EIGHT

Willingham states that young children are capable of engaging in reasoning and teachers are responsible for developing this skill.[4]

Beginning in preschool and certainly in elementary school, much of the focus of education in the classroom is on structure. Focusing on behavior management and rote learning sets the process for learning going forward. There is little attention on exploration of content, and limited questioning by students is allowed because the teacher must get through a core of information. The reality is that teachers are held accountable for the lack of "progress" among their students and therefore, the system dictates the structure of the classroom. Students must be at a certain point in the content memorization at the end of each school year or they may be held back. If this happens, the teacher may not be reviewed positively.

Although classroom management has changed somewhat over the recent decades, there remains an emphasis to sit quietly, stay in line, listen closely, and conform to classroom rules. These early years set the stage for high school and beyond. Students soon learn how to make it through the process, learning how to memorize and focusing on what is likely to be on a test. Coloring outside of the lines is not looked upon favorably. In fact, students that learn differently based on their ability to comprehend different communication techniques (auditory, visual, reading) may have greater difficulty in learning environments that do not utilize critical thinking.

There are exceptions to this traditional teaching process. There are teachers who make an effort to allow for individualization of learning and provide opportunities for interest focused exploration. However, even this is not enough. The need is to provide even very young minds with tools and techniques to explore and analyze basic information. Students need to be encouraged to question things and be asked questions that cause them to think differently about the value of a selected piece of information.

Young children do not need the higher order learning abilities of older students in order for teachers and others to begin to instill critical thinking concepts. Encouraging questioning, providing options, and evaluating content can be done early in the educational process even if in a limited manner.

There is a wide range of activities that can be used with young children. For example, using everyday life occurrences, young children can be asked why they think a person did what they did or what could they have done differently.

Reading simple passages in a book, children could be asked what they think that means and then what else could it mean (alternatives can be provided, especially initially to model the process).

They can work in groups to solve problems. With writing ability, they could be asked to write what they think and then have groups of four or five discuss their answers and arrive at a consensus.

Education is an opening of the mind to new ideas, new ways of thinking, and exploring the unknown. This is not accomplished if the level of "learning" and development is judged in terms of students making the right check marks on a multiple-choice test. This is the most basic of learning, rote memorization.

Here the focus is pointing out how the education system begins the process of content memorization from the first day of classroom instruction. Students can ask clarification questions or seek more information, but generally students are not encouraged to question what is presented by the teacher or written in a book. This is the foundation for future learning techniques. The pattern is set, and it takes a concerted effort to overcome the indoctrination process of the elementary school years.

There are things one must learn in these early years in order to function in our society. Certainly, there is content that must be taught and learned, but for the most part, it does not require memorization. What we need to remember will stay with us and be readily recalled. Basic skills for reading, writing, spelling, semantics, sentence structure are some of the fundamental skills that are taught through repetition but can be retained without overly focusing on memorization. Most information can be analyzed and questioned. In the early formative years, students should be encouraged to look beyond finite information provided in the classroom and be encouraged to question validity or minimally ask if there is more information than provided. Lead them to seek more and instruct them on how to do it.

It has been argued that young children are not ready for critical thinking and that the emphasis must be on content and memorizing the information provided. There is a necessary foundation of information as noted above; beyond that we need to be encouraging young children to think and analyze information. The building blocks for early learning can be taught in tandem with laying the foundation for critical thinking. It must be started early. If not done, it is difficult to overcome the ingrained "learning" process provided in schools at every level.

Students can be provided with age level questions to ask that are streamlined from what we expect of older students and logical concepts that are readily understandable even in the first grade and absolutely by the third grade. Here are some ideas to use with younger children.

In interactive situations such as incidents on the playground, teachers can provide students with suggestions on how to deal with them before reacting. This will likely reduce many problematic incidents. Teachers can provide scenarios to be discussed in the classroom as examples of verbal or behavioral confrontation or general interactions. Students can discuss what is going on and how it could be dealt with. Teachers can add comments to complete the analysis. Students should be encouraged to ask questions. They can learn to ask themselves questions such as why would the other person act or say something negative or hostile, how should they react, are there alternative actions, should they just walk away, should they engage in a nonconfrontational manner, should they ask questions to clarify the other person's behavior, and other similar thoughts. This will empower students to be interactive, understanding, and less reactive in these situations. This can be expanded to include a variety of situations. This can be tied into critical thinking generally. That is, encourage students to analyze situations before judging or reacting verbally or physically.

When students are reading or listening to something, they should be asking themselves similar questions: Why accept this information as accurate, where else can information be located about this, who can provide more information, did the person provide enough to assure me that the information is accurate and useful, and so on? This will prepare students to question information outside of the classroom and apply what they learned to a variety of situations.

If the process to create analytical thinking is not started at an early age it becomes more difficult later on in the educational process.

In several studies as part of a multidisciplinary research effort, psychologists conducted research with first and second graders and fifth and sixth graders. They found that students responded to questions incorrectly because there was information missing. The information they read did not contain an answer to some of the questions, but they answered them anyway. They did not analyze the information sufficiently (critically) to recognize they could not answer some of the questions asked.[5] This is interesting, because students assumed the answer was in the content they read; otherwise why was the question asked? Rather than question this, they selected one of the options. Had these students been taught to think critically they might have been more likely to recognize the lack of information to answer some of the questions and verbalized the concern to the teacher.

The process of teaching students to think critically can and should be implemented at an early age as it will serve them well in all aspects of their lives.

HIGH SCHOOL

The typical high school, according to Sizer, is "a place of friendly, orderly, uncontentious, wasteful triviality."[6] These are the years when students are preparing for college or a career upon graduation. The focus is on learning what one must know to pass a test to achieve the best grade possible and score high on college or technical school entrance tests. The hope for critical analysis or questioning content is further diminished.

If critical thinking is not infused in the early years of education, it is unlikely students will suddenly become critical thinkers when they enter high school. It will take a concerted effort to overcome prior learning expectations focused on memorization, but the effort needs to be made.

Despite the dominant focus of high school education being memorization of content, action must be taken to instill in teenagers a tenacity and drive to think for themselves. Additionally, the grading system is a process that fails to evaluate students' growth, can be self-defeating, and is not a measure of what students have learned but instead a measure, perhaps, of how they have been taught.

Lifelong learners need the tools to think and evaluate material. Teachers need to excite students about exploration, discourse, and analysis and stop focusing on memorization, preparation for tests, and advocating accepting of whatever is contained in textbooks at face value.

As Howard Gardner states, "The meat and potatoes of education should be learning to think. But what children are being served instead is a plateful of facts that don't add up to knowledge. What they need is training that will help them better understand why the world is as it is and how life can and should be lived. Instead, teachers are filling students with a lot of empty calories until their minds are bloated with facts."[7]

As students enter their teenage years, their ability to think abstractly and to reason at a higher order is expanding and they are able to assess and judge complex information. Unfortunately, in the education system in place, their first six years of education have blunted that potential and regimented the process of rote "learning."

Beginning during preadolescence, teachers should be opening the minds of students to enhance their ability to evaluate material and make decisions about what makes sense to them. They should be given the skills and tools to read differently by evaluating information and exploring options. Critical thinking is not advanced by telling students what to read, what to remember, and what will be on the test to make sure they prepare properly.

Given the state of education today, students are not as prepared as they could be for life after high school and participation in society. High schools are rated based on how well the student body does on standardized tests, how many go to college (especially the top-rated schools), and graduation rates. None of these rating factors speak to how well they can think and analyze issues or situations. How well are they prepared for the future when they no longer are in school, when they no longer have the "expert" to teach them, when they must make decisions and judgments on their own? Memorizing content does not prepare students for this. However, many "top-rated" high schools focus on content memorization and teaching material focused on getting high scores on college entrance examinations because it attracts parents who want their children to get into the "best" schools as well as businesses that want to be in top-rated communities.

High schools could give attention to college entrance exam expectations, while teaching students to think critically. Critical analysis will help students discern answers to complex questions via understanding how to analyze options and determine the best response. Critical thinking will expand potential to do well on these tests by arming students with skills to analyze and determine the correct response.

The ability to critically evaluate what a question is asking and then assess the possible responses will assist students to narrow the options to determine the answer or the best narrative response.

It is heartening to note that more and more colleges are eliminating standardized entrance exams in favor of other assessments which are more likely to determine college potential. Perhaps in the not-too-distant future, no students will be burdened with these narrow assessments.

COLLEGE

College is certainly the place for critical thinking to be encouraged, nourished, and emphasized. However, what students often receive is higher order content memorization.

Of course, a major difficulty is that students come to college already programmed to focus on content memorization. It takes considerable effort to reprogram them away from memorization and fact regurgitation toward critical thinking (problem solving, analysis, questioning, seeking alternatives, and how they read materials).

In this teacher's experience older students are much more amenable to critical thinking than those that had just graduated recently from high school. The older students have forgotten the regimentation of high school education and embrace this "new" way of learning. There are innumerable testimonials from older students who were pleased to have the opportunity to be in a classroom that opened their minds and encouraged them to think.

Many younger students also find these classes refreshing and challenging. Some struggled with this different way to deal with the content. They were not used to analyzing content they read and the different types of assessments to determine their critical thinking growth. Psychology classes bring a majority of students who are taking the class to meet a requirement for social science credits. Therefore, their interest in the content often is not strong at the beginning. They are seeking to find a class they can walk through with limited challenge and often not wanting to do more than is necessary to complete the requirement. Many do not understand why they should take the class since it has nothing to do with their major or the career they are pursuing.

This is the state of college education: students are primarily (only?) interested in courses that meet their career focus. Taking classes for the sake of broadening one's knowledge is of minimal interest. Many students have not developed an understanding that lifelong learning is predicated on a diversity of information not just their major interest. If they are confronted with a challenging new way to address content and while providing little of the structured routine they find comforting, they have difficulty. Changing teaching methods to focus on critical thinking with this caveat is challenging, but worth the effort.

Students in higher education are not necessarily seeking anything beyond content, focusing on getting through to a degree that will lead to a well-paying job. There is limited appeal for courses that do not focus on their goal. In a similar manner, teachers view their role as providing the content they think students need to prepare them for a career.

Many students then move on to graduate school where the content focus is even more pronounced. In graduate classes, teaching is focused on providing information to prepare students for careers. Graduate programs are designed to provide specific content without question or analysis to ensure students graduate with the requisite content to become practitioners or experts.

This citation from belle hooks sums up this perspective on college teaching, "In graduate school I found that I was often bored in classes. The banking system of education (based on the assumption that memorizing information and regurgitating it represented gaining knowledge that could be deposited, stored, and used at a later date) did not interest me. I wanted to become a critical thinker. Yet that longing was often seen as a threat to authority."[8]

A colleague of mine noted that he was in a doctoral program wherein there were a couple of courses wherein professors read sections from the textbook highlighting the importance of some narrow content. Certainly, by this level of education students should be capable of reading and understanding, but this was part of the professor's "teaching" method. No questioning, no expansion of material, just read the book, take tests, and complete the class.

Graduate school can be viewed as more educationally constricting than undergraduate school because of the emphasis on narrow ranges of content based on the area of interest in a specific field. This can mean another four or five years of information cramming with limited effort given to analysis or countering views. Although it is important to gain sufficient knowledge to be a practitioner in a specialty field, there is room (a need) for critical thinking that evaluates options and allows for discourse and clarification. Otherwise, it is not a learning environment that investigates ideas, but rather a closed process that contains only information deemed of value by the department and the teacher.

CAREERS

Students make it through high school, technical school or four to eight or more years of college, get their degrees, and move into their careers. They have the general content they need, but limited tools or developed skills to objectively analyze problems, seek different answers, or vary from the prescribed techniques.

On a purely intellectual ability (knowledge based level), graduating students are capable of problem solving in some fashion, but, for the most part, they have not been equipped with specific techniques to critically evaluate situations, actions, and information. Critical thinking is a skill and not just an automatic thought process. Most people naturally think "uncritically," making decisions based on the limited amount of information they have on any issue, personal biases, self-interest, or emotions. Everyone is vulnerable to thinking uncritically. Large percentages of employers complain that employees are unable to make choices without asking a supervisor. They are unable to make adjustments when confronted with unusual situations or problems because they have not been equipped to take such action.

The common refrain of employers is: "We need employees who can think, not just follow direction." The complaint is usually followed by an observation about how the world is changing too quickly to predict customers' demands, or that competitors are outpacing them. The only way to thrive, or even survive, these managers conclude, is to find workers who can be innovative, think outside the box, and make decisions on the spot. Neither high school nor college prepares them for this. When the classroom is devoted to memorization, there is limited time for questioning other than clarification and certainly no emphasis on critical thinking.

The same is true in a wide range of professional services that involve human interaction, such as medicine, accounting, social services, and more.

These professions need practitioners that are able to evaluate situations and react to differing cues in order to make the best judgments or decisions.

Not all surgeries are exactly the same even though they may involve the same human body part. Working with mental health issues or differing financial needs requires the ability to analyze and apply critical thinking skills to determine the issue and the best action to take.

Regardless of whether it is a manufacturing job, a medical profession, or rocket science there is a need for critical thinking and an ability to step back and analyze problems and nuances in order to make the best possible decision or take the best possible action.

SOCIETY, MEDIA, AND CULTURE

All aspects of life require critical thinking. Evaluating news content, candidates for office, deciding on issues of importance to families and other day to day living issues requires an ability to think critically to make the best decisions. Students graduate without any significant ability to detach themselves from the emotional aspect of material they read or hear, their biases, and the small knowledge they have to critically evaluate what they read, see, and hear. Consequently, they make decisions that may be all right, but often are not the best decision they could have made with proper assessment.

In recent years there has been a rapidly increasing development of information sources including social media, multiple news stations, blogs, and more. There is an information overload and it is very difficult to sort through it without some ability to think critically. It is paramount that we prepare children with critical thinking skills. If not, they are vulnerable to whatever media sources they access and may be misguided. Every day there are children tricked into risky or dangerous situations or are misinformed and believe things that are wrong and potentially hurtful. Schools are the best place for students to seek guidance and be provided with the analytical skills necessary to navigate this overwhelming information explosion.

THE CHALLENGE

This overview of education as students matriculate from preschool through high school describes issues about the state of education with regard to critical thinking. It reveals the overriding concerns and issues that make the effort to incorporate critical thinking in the classroom a challenge, but doable. It is emphasized that critical thinking must be woven into all aspects of course content and the entire learning process. It is of little impact if it is separated as something to know, but not fully integrated into the discussion of all content. Many schools, especially at the middle school and high school level, do have some critical thinking as part of the curriculum, but it is not sufficient. It will take time and effort, but it can be done. There is sufficient evidence indicating that if students are provided the opportunity early, they will thrive in this process of learning. It is more difficult when introduced later, but worth the effort. It takes commitment and the willingness of schools and teachers to deal with the pressure to provide a content focused classroom experience.

NOTES

1. Paul Preciado, *An Apartment in Uranus* (Los Angeles: Semiotext(e), 2019), 81.
2. Benjamin Bloom, bloomstaxonomy.net.
3. The Center for Critical Thinking, criticalthinking.org.
4. Daniel Willingham, *The Reading Mind* (Hoboken, NJ: Jossey-Bass, 2017), 44.
5. John Bransford, "Teaching Thinking and Problem Solving: Research Foundations," *American Psychologist* 41, no. 10 (1986), 1078–89.
6. Theodore Sizer, *Horace's Hope: What Works for the American High School* (Boston: Mariner Books, 1997), 17.
7. Howard Gardner, *The Disciplined Mind: The Education Every Child Deserves* (New York: Penguin, 1999), 56.
8. belle hooks, *Teaching to Transgress* (New York: Routledge, 1994), 94.

Chapter 3

Why Critical Thinking Is Essential

> Your education is worthless to you until you have lost your textbooks, burnt your lecture notes and forgotten the minutiae you memorized for examinations.
>
> —Alfred Whitehead, *The Aims of Education*

This quote is a strong statement, and many may think overstated. However, sometimes it is necessary to overstate a point in order for others to stop and pay attention. In the broad context of education, Whitehead's perspective simply stated is that the classroom should be more than reading textbooks and memorizing. It should challenge students to be curious, questioning, and relentless in the pursuit of knowledge.

In terms of developing skills for the twenty-first century focused on life-long learning critical thinking should be the core of all classroom teaching. This is a gradual process which requires effort and development over years. It should begin early before the routine of memorization becomes the only benchmark of learning.

General (liberal arts) education has always been more than just particular truths in a narrow range of fields. It aims to reveal the relevance of these truths, the connections, and relations among the particulars. Students should understand not just the truths but the search for truth; not just knowledge but the methods by which we acquire and confirm knowledge.[1] This amplifies the importance of how knowledge is gained and understood. It is not by memorization, but by use of logical principles and critical analysis.

Henderson and Dancy note that despite the recognized national need for the kind of problem-solving, critical-thinking risk-takers formed through the pedagogies of engaging students actively in the learning process, their adoption is not widespread. One significant barrier is breaking down the institutional culture of the educational process even though STEM faculty understand some of the problems with traditional ways of teaching. Henderson and

Dancy conclude that situational characteristics consistent with traditional instruction account for the major impediments. Their suggestion, directed at the broader STEM research community, is really for us all: identify both the situational barriers faculty face—bolted-down chairs, large enrollment classes, the need to "cover" content, student lack of experience with active learning, among others—and the means to removing those barriers. As they say, after all, getting the chairs unbolted is often a nontrivial task.[2]

The acquisition of knowledge is a collective process. It's not just a group of people commenting on each other's internet posts. It's a network of institutions—universities, courts, publishers, professional societies, media outlets—that have set up an interlocking set of procedures to hunt for error, weigh evidence, and determine which propositions pass muster.

These are the same principles as those of the scientific method. No one gets the final say (every proposition might be wrong). No claim to personal authority (who you are doesn't determine the truth of what you say, the evidence does). No retreat to safety (you can't ban an idea just because it makes you feel unsafe or conversely accept one because it does).[3]

Essentially, the why of critical thinking is it will help students and graduates make better decisions, analyze actions, determine more logical directions, avoid accepting false information, and function as better citizens.

It cannot be stated often enough that the most essential part of formal education is to teach people how to think, not what to think. Although most teachers agree with this, most have no idea how to implement critical thinking in the classroom, because schools of education do not provide the necessary education and training to undertake the process.

Yet research conducted with the Association of American Colleges and Universities found deficiencies focused on the ability of students to think critically. Critical thinking scores have shown the most need for improvement and have also provided the most useful information for curriculum change. Although not at all surprising, results from student work scored on critical thinking are the lowest across all learning goals. Within the dimensions of critical thinking, student performances were scored highest on explaining the issues, with over a third of the students able to clearly describe and clarify the issue to be considered, and another third of the students able to describe the issue, although with some information omitted. Students had the most difficulty identifying context and assumptions when presenting a position, and tying conclusions to a range of information, including opposing viewpoints and identifying consequences and implications. It is noted that "it also suggests that general education courses, in addition to courses in the majors, will likely need to stress critical thinking more in order for future graduates to attain capstone, or level 4, scores in critical thinking before graduation."[4]

From Elder's perspective, the reason teacher preparation programs fail to place critical thinking at the heart of the curriculum is twofold. First, the faculty who control and teach the curriculum simply do not know what critical-thinking is. Second, they think they do.[5]

Although it seems intuitive, critical thinking and engaging students in the process of evaluating material should be structured. There are logical principles, the Socratic Method, and other questioning techniques that define critical thinking.

Students who are explicitly taught to think critically also do better on subject-based exams and standardized tests than those who are not. In terms of developing twenty-first-century skills, including lifelong learning, teaching critical thinking should be the core effort. Most teachers have not been explicitly taught the intellectual skills inherent in critical thinking and teach it as though it is similar to rote memorization. They confuse schooling with intellectual development.[6]

As noted earlier the first benchmark for critical and independent thought is the Socratic Method, which is essential questioning that progresses via give and take. The individual offers a thought, and the listener questions it. More information is provided to justify the position and the other person questions that. The first person questions the second person's question, and the interchanges go back and forth until there appear to be no further questions to ask or no additional information to provide. This of course is the most basic initiation to critical and evaluative thought, challenging content with questions. More extensive examples for implementing critical thinking are provided in chapter 5.

There are of course numerous other techniques and ways to implement critical thinking. Here are other things that critical thinking emphasizes:

- Open-mindedness: Encourage students to avoid narrow thinking. Look for alternatives.
- Intellectual Curiosity: Probing, looking for inconsistencies.
- Clarification and Understanding: Inferences and conceptualization of ideas.
- Intellectual Carefulness: Checking accuracy, looking for errors, and thoroughness.
- Evaluation of Reasons: Seeking evidence for stated facts and assertions.
- Metacognitive Exploration: Analyzing thought processes and using different strategies.
- Problem Solving/Decision Making: Analyzing why decisions and problems were solved in specific ways. What else could be done.

"My worst mistakes as a teacher always came when I valued the content over the children. When I felt pressured to cover material rather than grow them as learners."[7] The author's college teaching career began with content teaching, but it was realized halfway through the first semester that this couldn't be done. Prior to the second semester the effort was to develop critical-thinking activities and materials to engage students in a way different from anything they had experienced.

If all instructors agreed that the quality of mental processing, not the production of correct answers, is the measure of educative growth, something hardly less than a revolution in teaching would be worked.[8] This is a citation from Dewey in the mid-twentieth century, but we have not done much to move in this direction in seventy-five years.

There is a direct relationship between teacher practices and student development of critical thinking. They essentially cannot do it on their own. Teachers are the single most important factor in developing critical-thinking skills in students.[9] This cannot be some add-on small portion of the curriculum, but rather the principal focus of all teaching in every classroom. If teachers do not do it, no one is likely to fill the void.

Unfortunately, even in schools that view critical thinking as "part" of the educational process, they do not see it as being utilized in all course work. That is, they see it as fitting into certain fields of study, but not others. Rarely introduced into the physical sciences or literature. They seem to think that it only fits in the "soft" sciences such as social sciences, philosophy, political science, and similar fields. This is wrong because it is equally important in every field of study since none are free from debatable ideas, theories, research, and other components. This is important if we are going to give credibility to critical thinking. It must be throughout the entire curriculum and implemented every day. As with any learning, if not repeated and utilized frequently it soon lies dormant and students revert quickly to their comfort zones of memorization and test taking.

Much of the implementation suggestions presented in this book focus on the author's teaching of psychology classes. However, the techniques and suggestions are implementable in any classroom with any content. There are many experts in critical thinking that offer techniques for implementation of the process.

At the beginning and again at the end of the semester the why of critical thinking for students was highlighted. This encompasses an approach to life that is far different than what is achieved in a content heavy, memorization focused classroom. The approaches to life which characterize part of the "why" of critical thinking from this perspective include:

1. Inquisitiveness regarding issues confronted.

2. Concern to become and remain well-informed.
3. Alertness to opportunities to use critical thinking.
4. Trust in the processes of reasoned inquiry.
5. Self-confidence in one's own abilities to reason.
6. Open-mindedness regarding divergent views.
7. Honesty in facing one's biases, stereotypes, and prejudices.
8. Prudence in suspending, making, or altering judgments.
9. Willingness to reconsider and revise views where reflection suggests change is warranted.
10. Using logical concepts and principles to aid in assessing information regardless of the source and apparent validity.

These are a few of the basic outcomes from teaching students to think critically. It goes beyond the classroom to all aspects of their lives. If we can provide them with the tools and techniques to evaluate information, they will be better prepared to be productive and informed citizens.

Students do not need teachers to help them read and memorize a book or other material. They do need teachers to guide them to evaluate material and prepare them for life outside of the classroom. One important value of providing these ten points early in the semester is students have a sense of the broader utility and value of critical thinking. When revisited at the end of the semester they leave armed with skills to address them.

Students were then provided the "how to accomplish this" during the many weeks of class. This is the focus of the next section. The point here is that critical thinking is not just an academic tool, but one that has utility throughout life in all aspects of what one does.

Using a broader perspective on the why and what of critical thinking these points provide insights:

- Start early: it's important to tailor the activity for the children's age, but it is possible to have them use their brains as early as possible.
- Do not answer their questions right away: teachers want to help students by giving them the answers so they can move on with the task, but if the main goal is to make them think, you may want to give them time to find the answers on their own. Alternatively, have them work in pairs or groups and try to find the answers together. That is not just an opportunity to foster collaboration, but you may be surprised at how creative your students get.
- Foster critical thinking by asking questions and having students think of the answers.
- Encourage students to think in new ways and to see different relationships with the same information.

- It is not just about science and facts. Critical thinking will make students intellectually aware of their own limited knowledge and the need to address different ideas constantly. Through research and reasoning, they will accomplish their tasks with integrity.
- These skills can be applied to discuss issues in math, literature, history, sociology, moral issues, or any content from any subject. Once developed, their use is limitless.[10]

The essence of this perspective is to start early and continuously foster critical thinking. Unfortunately, we are focused on test taking and not thinking.

Looking at outcomes of teaching critical thinking, there are innumerable citations highlighting its importance and value in all areas of life.

Kramer[11] considers that when an issue comes up in the workplace, the common reaction is to assume it falls into a predetermined category. However, critical thinking does not make any assumptions. It forces employees and managers to look beyond conventional solutions and seek new ideas to address problems.

A national survey of business and nonprofit leaders found:

- Nearly all employers surveyed (93%) say that "a demonstrated capacity to think critically, communicate clearly, and solve complex problems is more important than [a candidate's] undergraduate major."
- Even more (95%) say they prioritize hiring college graduates with skills that will help them contribute to innovation in the workplace.
- About 95 percent of those surveyed also say it is important that those they hire demonstrate ethical judgment and integrity; intercultural skills; and the capacity for continued new learning.
- More than 75 percent of those surveyed say they want more emphasis on five key areas including: critical thinking, complex problem solving, written and oral communication, and applied knowledge in real-world settings.[12]

One survey of employers found 59 percent strongly agree and another 37 percent somewhat agree that all college students should have educational experiences that teach them how to solve problems and seek and critically evaluate opposing views.[13]

These perspectives indicate how important independent critical thinking is in the workplace and how apparently lacking graduating students are to meet needs and expectations.

Butler, Pentoney, and Bong[14] state that critical-thinking skills are a far better indicator for making positive life decisions than raw intelligence. IQ scores leave a large portion of variance in predicting real-life behaviors. Critical thinking ability is a better predictor.

The Pearson Partnership[15] states that critical thinking can be improved with training and opportunity to think in real-life situations. It should start early, but it is never too late to implement critical-thinking strategies. Work environments can readily provide these opportunities.

In the workplace, classroom, or other life experiences, critically thinking is essential. That is why we must start early and provide guidance throughout the educational experience.

Perhaps nothing provides a more apparent need for critical thinking than the plethora and content in all media. We are bombarded daily with slanted views, omission of key information, repetition of self-serving proclamations, and similar roadblocks to clarity. Most people read and view a small array of content providers and rarely take time to listen to countering views. Even those that do likely do not change their own entrenched positions based on long developed biases. Few people take the time to step back and analyze the information they receive from all outlets. If it fits their narrow perspective, they accept it. If not, they reject it. Not much room for assessment and determination of what may or may not be correct. Much of what fits an individual's thinking about any issue is based on early learning and building upon that to support the foundation. People have not been taught to think critically and seek alternative views. Rather they learned from teachers, parents, and others a certain body of knowledge, positions, and actions and they personally reinforce them daily without thinking about their validity or whether there is other information or positions with equal or more validity. Some summary thoughts on the importance of logical thinking in the classroom come from Benjamin Bloom, an educational psychologist.

The next several paragraphs paraphrase a section of his writing on the understanding and use of logic.

Many in the educational field have conceptualized the acquisition and retention of knowledge as having many domains or levels of depth.

The first domain is remembering. In essence, it refers to retaining facts. Unfortunately, retaining facts without understanding them is of little value. It also has a very limited life span.

The next level is comprehension or understanding. This is shown by our ability to express in our own words the meaning of the information.

With understanding, we can start to analyze, catalog, or break down the knowledge; to judge, appraise, or evaluate the knowledge; and to relate it to a new context, or to synthesize by integrating it with other information. This requires critical thinking and an understanding of the logical principles for analyzing content.

When learning many skills in law, medicine, and other areas of study, it is critical that we have the ability to use the knowledge that has been acquired. Without this ability, the facts by themselves have limited worth.

The term logic is commonly used to describe codes of good reasoning. It used to be a subject taught in schools. But now it is rarely formally taught. Informal logic is sometimes described as critical thinking. It tells us how people reason things out, figuring out whether the conclusions follow the assumptions.

Formal logic is the systematic and organized application of the principles of logic. The principles of logic are universal and apply to all fields.

Both types of logic are needed, and educational institutions must emphasize logical reasoning in all areas of study.[16]

Unfortunately, many see the use of logical principles and thinking too difficult or not applicable in many instances. Of course, this is incorrect. How can thinking logically not be applicable in any situation? For some the formal concepts may seem stodgy and dated, but they are no less relevant today than they were during Socrates' time.

Without logical reasoning people tend to think and react emotionally or only utilize existing understanding or knowledge. Without questioning and submitting information or content to the scrutiny of logic, how do people know it is correct or the only possible answer? This question is purposely left open to ponder.

NOTES

1. Principles of Mathematics and Logic: A Course for Liberal Arts Students, R.A.G. Seely Mathematics Department, John Abbott College, Ste Anne de Bellevue, QC 2020.

2. Charles Henderson and Melissa H. Dancy, "Barriers to the Use of Research-Based Instructional Strategies: The Influence of Both Individual and Situational Characteristics," *Physical Review Physics Education Research* 3, no. 2 (2007): 26.

3. Jonathan Rauch, *The Constitution of Knowledge: A Defense of Truth* (Brookings Institution Press, 2021), 62.

4. Linda Siefer, "Assessing General Education Learning Outcomes," *Peer Review* (Fall/Winter 2011): 9–12, https://www.nyu.edu/content/dam/nyu/academicAssessment/documents/2014AcademicAssessmentSymposium/Peer%20Review_Vol%2013(4)_Assessing%20Liberal%20Education%20Outcomes%20Using%20VALUE%20Rubrics.pdf. Research done with the Association of American Colleges and Universities.

5. Linda Elder, criticalthinking.org.

6. Peter Ellerton, Creative Commons, January 2020, https://creativecommons.org/2019/12/09/save-the-date-public-domain-day-2020-is-happening-in-january-in-washington-d-c/.

7. Shanna Peeples, *Think Like Socrates* (Thousand Oaks, CA: Corwin Press, Inc., 2019), 73.

8. John Dewey, *The Later Works of John Dewey, 1949–1952*, vol. 16 (Carbondale, IL: SIU Press, 2008), 28.

9. Linda Elder, criticalthinking.org.

10. Ana Tatsumi, "Teaching Critical Thinking in the Language Classroom," *World of Better Learning* (blog), April 4, 2018, https://www.cambridge.org/elt/blog/2018/04/04/teaching-critical-thinking/.

11. Lindsay Kramer, "What are the Benefits of Critical Thinking in the Workplace," Chron.com, July 2020.

12. Scott Jaschik, "Well Prepared in Their Own Eyes," insidehighered.com, January 2015.

13. Hart Research Associates, "It Takes More than a Major: Employer Priorities for College Learning and Student Success" (April 2013), 1–15, https://dgmg81ph-hvh63.cloudfront.net/content/user-photos/Research/PDFs/2013_EmployerSurvey.pdf. Research survey done on behalf of the Association of American Colleges and Universities.

14. Heather A. Butler, Christopher Pentoney, and Mabelle P. Bong, "Predicting Real-World Outcomes," *Thinking Skills and Creativity* 25 (2017): 84.

15. Anisa Zulfiqar, "The Importance of Teaching Critical Thinking to Students," *Pearson Partnership* (blog), June 30, 2018, https://www.talentlens.com.au/blog/teaching-critical-thinking-to-students.

16. Benjamin Bloom, *Taxonomy of Educational Objectives: The Classification of Educational Goals* (Harlow, UK: Longman, 1971), 13.

Chapter 4

Educational Transformation

> I am passionate about everything in my life—first and foremost, passionate about ideas. And that's a dangerous person to be in this society—not because I'm a woman, but because it's such a fundamentally anti-intellectual, anti-critical-thinking society.
>
> —belle hooks, onwisconsin.uwalumni.com, Spring 2022

A strong statement from hooks that may offend some and be dismissed by others. However, a reasonably objective view of America might arrive at the same conclusion. The general population tends to be suspect of the ivory tower and those "removed" from the worwkaday world. We glorify action rather than thinking. We prefer making decisions to contemplating options. We prefer answers to uncertainty.

After years of education, it was not until my sophomore year at the University of Wisconsin that I found a teacher challenging traditional learning techniques and providing methods of thinking that required no formal memorization of "facts" but rather analysis of what was read. Dr. Michael Hakeem, sociology professor, at UW is the singular most important teacher in my long academic career. If not for Dr. Hakeem, I would have been mired in the same mundane rote memorization of content learning without analysis as provided in all other classes I attended. He was a beacon of light that transformed my thinking about learning and the educational process.

Dr. Hakeem was a unique teacher. He was not publishing books, giving lectures around the country, or doing anything more than focusing on teaching and enlightening students in how to think for themselves and seek answers beyond the textbook and lectures. Classes were not lectures, but rather a continual review of material, questioning, demanding validity, seeking other perspectives, never allowing students to be content with one answer. These classes made students wary of "celebrity" among academicians who enjoyed the limelight more than the pursuit of teaching in the classroom. Students were cautioned about listening to speeches offered by any individual with notoriety because there is a tendency to be taken in by presentation style rather than listening and evaluating the content of what is being said. Dr. Hakeem encouraged students to read materials these individuals published to avoid being taken in by presentation style rather than the content of what is being said by the speaker. Dr. Hakeem is gone, and dearly missed.

Here is an example of Dr. Hakeem's teaching style. Students were directed to ask him a question about anything in the realm of sociology. Dr. Hakeem would walk to one side of the stage and provide an elongated answer. Then another student was directed to ask the same question and Dr. Hakeem would walk to the other side of the stage and give a completely different answer. Both answers were supported by citations of "experts" in the field. It was truly spellbinding to listen to this gifted teacher continually provide contrasting answers or at least different perspectives for the same question. Students were left to decide for themselves, but more importantly, to do research on the topic to gain more insight to the issue. This is education and it instills in students the drive to think for themselves. From that point forward, my pursuit has been to always seek different perspectives and question why whatever is offered is the prevailing answer. Predominantly to analyze and look for flaws in the logic of the position taken or the information provided.

During multiple classes with Dr. Hakeem, we were never tested on memorized content. We were never told this is one answer. Our work in his classes was to find differing perspectives and evaluate the information to determine which point of view (or views) we could defend as the most logical based on our analysis. It was challenging and exhilarating. A breath of fresh air from the routine of every other class.

The following two chapters provide the specifics of the process and details for implementing critical thinking in the classroom. Although the critical thinking techniques are broadened beyond what Dr. Hakeem offered in order to incorporate other critical thinking activities, it is difficult to replicate the expanse of Dr. Hakeem's ability to evaluate material and help students to be critical thinkers. The effort is worth it because when students exit the course at the end of a semester they are far better equipped to think and evaluate than they were when they entered.

Similar assessment techniques are used for all topics, theories, issues, and so forth. In the field of psychology an important issue is the effectiveness of various treatment modalities. For example, there are multiple schools of thought regarding treatment techniques and anticipated results. In the classroom, if the teacher is behaviorally focused, the students would be told that the most effective treatment emphasizes analyzing patient behavior. This entails having the patient define their behavior and then a treatment plan is developed that is based on their actions and how to modify those actions in a positive manner. The behaviorist treatment model is essentially to have the patient tell the therapist their concern and describe the behavior. Then the therapist provides the person with techniques to change the behavior pattern.

If the teacher is psycho-dynamically oriented, given the same patient the treatment modality focuses on causation. This modality emphasizes the origin of the behavior and how to rebuild from that point. This theory states that knowing the cause of the problem will lead to resolution and improvement.

These two treatment modalities are at loggerheads. The first does not need to know the cause, just describe the behavior and the person will be provided with suggestions to change that behavior. The second states that it is critical to know the underlying cause for the behavior before a treatment plan can be devised. In a critical thinking classroom, both theories and others are presented, and the discussion focuses on analyzing them for similarities and differences and then determining the strengths and weaknesses as well as the overall value of each. This comparison process provides students with a clear understanding of why stating one theory or one position should be questioned.

It is unlikely that students know the focus of the teacher and, therefore, assume what the teacher is presenting is the best or predominant theory. This is not teaching, but rather "forced" learning of the teacher's bias. This is the same concern for whatever content is being taught. Students are unaware that the bias of the teacher may slant the information that is being provided. Even if the teacher offers several theories, the likelihood is they will emphasize one more than the others. This is a serious concern in graduate schools wherein the teacher and the department feel they are to produce practitioners and therefore they must be "educated/indoctrinated" to their preferred treatment modality.

This, of course, is the case in any field of study wherein graduate programs are expected to produce practitioners focused on their school's orientation regardless of the content or the fact that there are other equally (perhaps better) schools of thought. For example, in economics there are several major schools of thought and different graduate schools will be known for their orientation toward one over others. Is this education or indoctrination? Does this necessarily produce the best practitioners?

A class implementing critical thinking is different. Despite the teacher's preferences based on what college and graduate schools were attended and years of experience, it is not the teacher's role to indoctrinate students to what the teacher believes is correct. Rather it should be to open the field to students and encourage them to decide their direction based on an objective and evaluative presentation of a broad array of information.

This can and should be done in all fields of study and must certainly be done in general survey courses. It takes work to do this, but if teachers are truly educators, then this is what needs to be done.

It is also emphasized that students must determine what makes sense to them. Their thinking is questioned by the teacher, not to change their minds, but rather ensuring they have perspective and have evaluated other possibilities. The student is the focal point of this educational process, not the teacher, textbook, or test assessment. The teacher is the guide.

OVERVIEW OF TEACHING PROCESS

Essentially, other books on critical thinking provide generalized techniques that do not relate to specific course content or classroom structure. They are designed as an adjunct to the process of teaching. What this process does is introduce techniques, ideas, and other critical thinking actions that utilize the assigned textbook and allied materials, but in a unique manner. What is provided are methods to analyze and critically evaluate the course content that teachers have always used. This is not a separate process, used now and then; it is an integral part of the learning experience.

The teacher using critical thinking is not in the classroom to lecture but rather to guide students through material and engage them in the analysis and discussion process. The classroom is not competitive in the sense that no student's grade is dependent on how others did, but rather it is based on the teacher's knowledge of what students can achieve with the various assignments. In this sense, everyone can do well or not well or somewhere in between based on what could be achieved regarding their individual effort, critical analysis expectations, and other criteria that do not require comparison to other students.

The classroom is a cooperative endeavor wherein students work together with the teacher to enhance their learning. The teacher's role is to guide not lecture, engaging students in discussions. When introducing new information, it is always within the context of interactive discussion. Students are encouraged to ask questions and actively participate in expanding or narrowing the content provided. It is an interesting and challenging place to be and one that students enjoy entering. By the end of the semester, they view the learning process much differently than when they entered.

Regardless of the field of study, every course content needs to be evaluated, analyzed, questioned, and alternatives offered. It may initially seem prohibitive or not worth the effort, but as you read through the information and processes in the next chapter, give thought to how it could be adapted to any classroom and how it might change the classroom environment and be more fulfilling for teachers as well as students. Teaching using critical thinking as the integral part of all learning causes every class to be a challenge, because it is not possible to predict how students will react nor the flow of content and discussion. The teacher is learning along with the students.

Challenging students to think, question everything that is stated, and look beyond the textbook should be an essential part of the classroom experience. It requires the teacher to be open to challenging material, providing an array of sources and motivating students to think for themselves. Students will retain content and be knowledgeable of some of the broad array of information in the field of study, but they will also be questioning, looking for ways to expand on what they learned, and be open to new information whether it supports their thinking on a topic or issue.

To implement critical thinking in the classroom, teachers must be prepared to give up the comfort of lecturing, not rely on textbooks as the exclusive or principal source of information, and open the classroom to the excitement of intellectual inquisitiveness and exploration.

The next chapter provides the foundation materials for introducing critical thinking in the classroom. The following chapter overviews the specific implementation techniques.

Chapter 5

Teaching Students to Think
The Foundation

> It is not what you are taught, but how you are taught that causes the harm.
>
> —Jerry Farber, *The Student as N . . . er*

Farber is blunt, but this brief and pointed statement sums up the concern in our educational system. There is a wide expanse of content available, but the system from first grade through graduate school is focused on what is determined to be the most important information based on what is contained in textbooks or a relatively small array of other materials. More importantly, the concern is with how it is presented and what the expectations are for retention.

American students rank among the lowest of industrialized nations in math and science achievement as well as most other academic rankings.[1] Among a host of causes for this, one key reason is because the teaching process focuses on memorization of data and information acquisition without complementary awareness of understanding, investigating, and evaluating the data and other content. A significant amount of classroom time in the United States is focused on content and memorizing "facts," which may not actually be "factual" or may not be agreed upon by others. These "facts" may be replaced by "new facts" in the future, without any regard for understanding why these are the "facts" and what alternative viewpoints may exist.

American students graduate from high school and college with a core of "facts" but limited ability to solve problems, analyze issues, or weigh differences in various content. They are not prepared to think. To overcome our educational deficits internationally, educational institutions in America need to develop students to be critical thinkers, developing their ability to evaluate conclusions and determine for themselves why to accept or reject a point of view regardless of the source. This will enhance creative analysis, problem solving, and integrative thinking as well as make them better citizens. Even though there may be some aspects of critical thinking introduced currently, it is a small piece of the educational effort. Critical thinking should not be an adjunct portion of the classroom experience, but rather woven into the educational process and all content.

Implementing critical thinking in the classroom will involve changing the teaching process and how content is utilized. The information in this chapter provides the foundation for implementing critical thinking as an integral part of the classroom experience.

Although focused on college teaching, this same learning process can be used in a modified manner at every level of education, by parents to help their children with everyday living experiences and employers with job duties, change needs, and growth. Enhancing critical thinking and analytical skills is useful in all walks of life. Schools and teachers must be the leaders.

The three sections on the following pages are provided to students during the first class to lay the foundation for the semester. They provide an overview of why critical thinking is important. The logical principles descriptions provided are universally applicable in the classroom and in everyday life. The types of research questions, classroom exercises, article assessments, discussion topics, and variance in how to read everything is adaptable regardless of course content. The focus is on thinking, questioning, analyzing, and engaging students to take charge of their education, not be passive participants expecting teachers to provide them with the knowledge they need with limited effort to explore and question.

WHY CRITICAL THINKING

There are many reasons why critical thinking is important to students and people in general. Here are four that relate to educational endeavors.

1. Everyone needs to think critically to be well-educated. The ability to see beyond the obvious or generally accepted answers, and to determine the validity of ideas is essential to learning and developing a breadth of knowledge.
2. Everyone needs to think critically to be competitive in the job market. With job performance expectations continually changing, the ability to think, evaluate options, and adapt to new opportunities are more important than any specific skill or information memorized in high school or college.

3. Everyone needs to think critically to deal with the information explosion. The amount of information available is doubling every few years. Not all of this new information is correct, beneficial, or useful. The information explosion can be overwhelming and without knowledge of the skills and techniques to evaluate it and make judgments, we can be lost in this myriad of content and opinion.
4. Everyone needs to think critically in all aspects of life, because we are continually confronted with ideas that need to be evaluated. To solve problems, it is invaluable to have critical thinking skills.

Depending on the content of the course, teachers may utilize some or all of the components in their implementation of critical thinking and logical reasoning in their classrooms.

Overall, the focus of each semester is to critically examine the textbook and other content, opinions, and research, and seek and compare alternatives. This teaching process is to move students away from thinking that everything in a textbook or other source is correct. There are alternative ideas that may be equally (more?) correct or at least call into question the validity of the material they read in the textbook or other sources.

CRITICAL THINKERS DEFINED

What makes one a critical thinker? What skills, knowledge, techniques, attitudes, and motivations do you need to effectively think critically, and analyze situations and content efficiently? Here are some guidelines to assist everyone along the road to being a critical thinker.

1. *Critical Thinkers Are Flexible*: They tolerate ambiguity and uncertainty. They are open-minded and refrain from either-or thinking on complex questions. Critical thinkers are willing to question their ideas and look for flexibility in the thinking of others as they present their ideas.
2. *Critical Thinkers Identify Inherent Biases and Assumptions*: This does not mean that statements that have bias are wrong, but we must be alert to the possibility. Be aware of vested interests in positions taken or statements made by others (how does the position benefit them). Look for potential biases in the thinking of others as they present their ideas (their background, work focus, education, social groups, political alliances, and more can impact how people view things and the positions they take).
3. *Critical Thinkers Are Skeptical*: This does not mean being skeptical merely because it does not fit your preconceived notions of something.

However, everyone should be disciplined and encouraged to question the statements and claims of others as well as their own. Look for whether, or not, others question their own ideas. The author is sometimes cynical as well as skeptical because of the inherent biases people exhibit with limited substance to support their views. Sometimes it is difficult to be objective when the views presented seem obviously wrong, but the discussion must be focused on objectivity not personal feelings or personal biases.

4. *Critical Thinkers Separate Facts from Opinions*: Too often there is a preference to rely on personal experiences rather than scientific data (especially in psychology and other social sciences). It is important to be emotionally detached when dealing with difficult issues in order to be open to "facts" or ideas that are different from personal opinions. Look for how well others present valid evidence for their positions. If their view is substantiated with evidence that appears well developed, it will be more acceptable than opinions that seem to be drawn from loosely developed research or analysis.

5. *Critical Thinkers Draw Logical Inferences*: This means that everyone needs to evaluate the logic in the presentations of others. Look for whether, or not, there are inconsistencies in their presentations (conclusions or ideas do not logically follow). Everyone jumps to conclusions at times, often with limited supportive information. Many decisions are based on information that supports personal thinking or fits into how individuals view things rather than being supported by verifiable research and/or data.

6. *Critical Thinkers Do Not Oversimplify*: Simple explanations are appealing, but often too simplistic to be correct. More often, complex causation is involved rather than a simple one-dimensional idea. It is important to look beyond what may seem obvious and seek alternatives. This is difficult since most of our educational experiences emphasize one answer, and work lives seek quick solutions to complex situations. Politicians are masters at oversimplifying answers to complex problems. Look for other possible explanations for conclusions reached by others and/or why theirs may be faulty.

7. *Critical Thinkers Examine Evidence*: It is important to look at diverse sources of information before determining a conclusion. By doing this it is possible to sort through and locate the best answer or answers. Look for whether, or not, others have relied on only one piece of information to draw conclusions. Of course, it is not always possible to be exhaustive in this effort, but certainly more than one piece of evidence would be of value to broaden perspectives before reaching conclusions.

A key concern is how to engage students in the process of critical thinking wherein it becomes enlightening and enjoyable to read differently, to understand why much of what they read is arguable and the effort it will take to find answers that make sense to them and hold up to evaluative scrutiny. The process of critical analysis and thinking becomes part of how they read, listen, and learn.

OBSTACLES TO CLEAR THINKING: USING LOGICAL PRINCIPLES

The obstacles to clear thinking form the basis for critical thinking because they arm students with logical principles to address numerous fallacies they may have overlooked in the past. Below is a short list of logical principles (there are dozens) with examples that are used throughout the semester in a variety of ways. This is the foundation document for critical thinking and analysis.

When reading material or listening to speakers, it is easy to be swayed by the ability of the individual to present information. Rather than evaluating what is being written or stated, often acceptance or not is based on presentation style. That is, speakers use a variety of techniques to convince the listener of their point of view and thereby shut down analysis (clear thinking). Of course, writers also can sway the reader, but at least the cult of personality and vocal energy are not part of the concern. When one reads there is not the emotional sway from the speaker or visual components that cause one to more readily accept information.

There are innumerable examples of orators who convinced their audiences of the correctness of their views based on the energy of their presentation and ability to convey their thoughts even though the content was suspect at best. George Wallace and Jim Jones are easy examples that used the power of delivery and engagement to convince people to follow them. If people would read what speakers were saying without the emotion of the vocal presentation it is less likely they would be swayed by the content provided.

If one is taught to see the logical fallacies it will be easier to be an objective listener. However even then it is more difficult when feeling the energy of the speaker. To be a "student," an "employee," and a "citizen" it is essential to have tools and skills to evaluate the content of information being presented in books, newspapers, television, radio, and so on, as well as by politicians and experts trying to convince you of something.

Few things are more important to students' education than the need to think independently, critically, and evaluatively. For it is not what you know, but how you gained the information and your ability to evaluate it. Once students begin to think critically, they will rarely (never?) just accept the pronouncements of "experts," whether in print or speech, without critical evaluation of the information they are providing. Asking questions is a principal part of learning. These obstacles to clear thinking are used throughout the semester to evaluate material in the book, articles provided, and information presented in discussions on specific topics.

1. Post hoc Fallacy:

This implies that the result that follows a specific action may have been caused by something other than the stated action. That is, merely because something follows after an action does not mean that the action caused the second event to occur. One must determine if other variables could have caused the stated result.

Example: To give students an example, a hypothetical study is provided wherein one group of teachers are given student test results indicating the level of placement for each student and another group of teachers are not given test results for student placement in class. Both groups were told that they had students that were below average, average, and above average and they could move students between groups during the year as they thought best based on student performance. At the end of the year, teachers without test results moved students around among the three groups more frequently while teachers that had test results indicating placement level at the beginning did not move students as readily among the three groups. The conclusion is that teachers given test scores will not go against the results because if they are wrong, they will not be viewed well and might be questioned as to why they did not rely on the test results. Teachers with no test scores did not have this constraint so they did move them. Therefore, it is better to not be constrained by test results.

This is a potential post hoc fallacy because it assumes a causal relationship that may not exist. With test results, few changes. No test results, more changes. However, another conclusion could be that the teachers without test results were not able to judge student performance well enough initially and therefore moved students around as they viewed performance. The test results may have been good, and students mostly properly placed, and the teachers did not need to make changes. One could reach either of these conclusions which are diametrically opposed from the same research result.

2. Emotional Appeals and Value Judgment:

In almost everything one reads or listens to, there are words that are designed to appeal to emotions or make value judgments based on the writer's or speaker's biases or opinions. This prevents individuals from objectively evaluating the content of ideas and deciding the value of the information. These words can be critical, uplifting, humorous, or just embellishing a point of view with adjectives. They may be just a personal opinion to influence people. Examples include words such as excellent, noteworthy, interesting, well-researched. Be aware of these influencers. The listener or reader should determine their value.

Example: "Behavior therapy is wrong because it relies on controlling you and how you act. It removes your personal control over what you do. This may work with animals in a laboratory, but we should not do this with humans." This is an appeal to the emotions of humans who do not want to be controlled but rather maintain self-determination. It is also a value judgment in that it presupposes this is bad or wrong. The statement offers no supportive information, but rather it relies on demonizing a treatment technique without evidence.

3. Non sequitur:

This implies that the conclusion reached does not necessarily follow from the premise. That is, although the premise is generally correct, there may be other conclusions than the one offered. The premise may also be faulty, but the key is that the conclusion is not the only possibility. Determine what other conclusions could be reached from the same premise other than the stated conclusion.

Example: People who are psychotic act in a bizarre manner. This person acts in a bizarre manner, therefore this person is psychotic. Although the premise may be correct, it does not follow that every person that acts in a bizarre manner is psychotic. This could just be an unusually behaving individual. Another example is that behaviorists focus on modifying behavior and how to help the person change, therefore those who believe in behavior modification obviously want to control everyone via rewards and punishments. The conclusion does not necessarily follow from the premise. Another conclusion is the behaviorist wants the individual to take personal control by using behavioral techniques that will promote change.

4. No Evidence or No Footnote:

If someone offers a viewpoint that requires information to support it, there should be a footnote, evidence provided, or a statement that this is an opinion. Someone's opinion does not have to be justified necessarily, but if they are implying there is support for their position or others should accept it because of who they are, they should offer a footnote or specific evidence with a footnote or state a source. A footnote constitutes evidence by providing a source, but actual supportive data is better. Note that validity is not determined by a footnote or information provided, but rather by the quality of the information/research.

Example: This one seems self-explanatory. It is an everyday occurrence. Whenever someone offers a viewpoint that needs a reference or supportive documentation that is not offered, it should be questioned and/or discounted.

5. Begging the Question or Faulty Assumptions:

Often, information will be presented that assumes that prior information or a prior question has already been agreed upon or proven. Additionally, sometimes the faulty assumption is that there are techniques to adequately conduct the research to arrive at the conclusions presented.

Example: Psychotherapy cures psychological impairments, therefore it should be used with all individuals with psychological issues. This is begging the question because it assumes the first part of the sentence to be correct and then concludes that it should be used widely. It must be proven that it does "cure" before the conclusion can be reached and certainly that it can be used for all types of psychological impairments. Among experts in psychology, there is broad disagreement regarding the impact of psychotherapy versus other therapies.

6. Oversimplification of a Complex Issue:

This involves stating an obvious or single reason for something that may have many other variables involved. The one reason stated may be correct, but it may not be the only reason or even the main reason and thus oversimplifies the resolution.

Example: During the war activity in the Middle East, a common chant was no blood for oil. This was catchy and achieved impact, but it oversimplified a complex geopolitical action that was far more involved than stated by this single issue. Although many may agree with this single conclusion, other reasons for the United States being there may have been more important.

7. Samples of One:

A sample of one is not sufficient to prove a point. We should be skeptical when someone offers a descriptive example of one individual, instance, or action to prove a point regarding general behavior of a group or an individual. We can find an example of one for essentially anything. Perhaps a single piece of research with a reasonable sample size may or may not be sufficient, but it is not a sample of one. However, a sample of one is acceptable when someone makes an all or none statement and a contrary example of at least one can be offered.

Example: The election of Barack Obama as president proves that racial discrimination is minimal in this country. One incident even of this magnitude does not prove this point conclusively.

8. Appeal to Ignorance:

This is especially of concern in the classroom wherein the teacher pronounces something as a fact and challenges students to refute it when for the most part they lack the knowledge to do so.

Example: "Freudian theory is the most reliable treatment modality because of the expanse of research and the number of practitioners using psychoanalytic techniques." If a student asks how the teacher knows this for a fact, the teacher asks the student to disprove it, which of course they cannot and therefore the teacher must be right. Merely because someone does not have an alternative to your view does not mean you are correct.

9. Ad hominem:

This is attacking or labeling the individual. Often you will find that the writer or speaker is attacking another person on a personal level rather than addressing the issues. You do not want to know what is wrong with the individual, but rather, what is wrong with their ideas, research, conclusions. This is discounting the person's views based on labeling or supposed lack of knowledge.

Example: The writer is not a physician and therefore they cannot write about medical issues. This, despite the fact that the writer did years of research on medical issues citing physicians and others. This is attacking the person for who they are not the validity of their content.

10. Vague Words:

This refers to words that do not provide sufficient clarity to the point being made. Words such as "many, suggests, several, few." Vague terms soften the point being made and leave it open to question.

Example: Many psychologists support the view that an eclectic approach to treating various mental illnesses is the best approach rather than focusing on one technique. How many and who are these psychologists and why is their view preferred to others who think a specific approach is better? Also, which cluster of treatment techniques should be used out of the innumerable theories that have been put forward?

11. Either-Or Argument:

This involves statements that are all or nothing in their evaluation of something. Such statements do not allow for a range of options or some blending of the opposing views.

Example: Psychological impairments are caused by either inherited traits or traumatic experiences. Why must it be one of these two? Are there other possibilities such as learned behaviors, physical impairments, conditioning, or other environment possibilities, or a combination of these?

12. Vested Interest:

Does the writer or speaker have a vested interest in the outcome, or the position taken? Will they or their group benefit in some manner based on their results or the position they are taking? Does this potentially cloud or influence the outcome or opinion they provide?

Example: A study was conducted by the Family Channel. The results indicated that television shows on other channels which show violence and criminal activity increase the potential for viewers to commit similar acts. These results are questionable because the organization funding the research has a vested interest in the outcome; namely, watch our channel because it does not have violence and criminal behavior.

13. Relevance:

Often one wonders about the relationship of the individual or content to the issue presented. This may be in the form of the credibility of the reference, the likelihood that the person or group cited in defense of a position does not have sufficient knowledge to offer a valid position, or the information does not seem to fit the point being made.

Example: The quoting of celebrities or others with limited understanding of complex issues can lead to many population segments making wrong decisions or not seeking other informational resources. How relevant is their opinion on an issue which requires complex knowledge?

14. Issues with Type of Research:

Are there concerns with the type of research used to support the conclusions that may call into question the stated results? These types of research include self-report with surveys, observer bias with observations, and over control with experiments. Analyze the research in terms of methodology, potential concerns with who conducted it, and the ability to conduct relevant research

Example: Polling research prior to elections is often used as conclusive information with little regard for sampling techniques, likelihood of certain populations being more or less responsive, and other sampling issues. Hillary Clinton was projected by all polls to win the election in 2016, yet she lost. It was thought at the time that these polls may have reduced Clinton voting turnout since the projections for her winning were strong.

15. Appeal to Authority:

When questioned, a person offers an authority that is in agreement and based on this the position should be accepted.

Example: B. F. Skinner states that it is best to focus on observable patient behavior rather than feelings or emotional content when offering treatment advice. If this is questioned, the person asks how you can refute an expert in the field, which of course most students would have difficulty doing. Merely because the questioner is not an authority and one is being cited, does not mean they cannot question a position. Because the person does not have an alternative does not make the position stated correct. Anyone can question things even if they are not an expert. It should cause the person with the position to assess it and maybe modify their view.

With this foundational information, the next chapter provides the details of how critical thinking is implemented in the classroom with an emphasis on using the obstacles to clear thinking and critical analysis.

NOTE

1. Drew DeSilver, "U.S. Students' Academic Achievement Still Lags That of Their Peers in Many Other Countries," Pew Research Center, February 2019, https://www.pewresearch.org/fact-tank/2017/02/15/u-s-students-internationally-math-science/.

Chapter 6

Implementation of Critical Thinking

The Hammes Classroom Experience

> Without instruction in critical thinking, students are apt to make blunders because the human mind tends toward undisciplined thinking. Critical thinking helps students transcend those habitual thinking patterns and helps them pinpoint connections and differences in concepts.
>
> —Robert Hutchins, The Center for Critical Thought

Hutchins sums it up well: it is paramount to teach critical thinking in order to enhance the potential for students to separate fact from fiction, analyze options, determine the best course of action, and be prepared for unexpected situations. These are skills that should be taught in the classroom for they are not spontaneously developed without guidance.

The experience of learning and retaining content using critical thinking and analysis is challenging and rewarding. The Hammes Classroom Experience (hereafter HCE) provides the details of how to implement critical thinking in college classrooms. This can be readily adapted in some manner at all levels of education and in all other areas of life.

The focus of the initial class periods is on acclimating students to a different way of learning. Students are provided with materials that provide descriptive information regarding critical thinking and the use of logical principles as the driver. This is accomplished by using content from the textbook, other resources, and materials students are instructed to source and bring to class. Although there is a textbook, students need to get beyond the book and find other sources on any given topic. There are no in class tests, no memorization, and no pushing of one perspective over another.

Before students leave the class at the end of the semester, they are able to find the library (and source properly on the internet), find relevant material, and know what to do with the material once they have it (which is the most essential component). Initially this may be difficult for students because it is unfamiliar, but when comfortable with the process it is exciting and invigorating. It opens a new world for them and brings new energy to their learning. Memorizing names, dates, and other information can be mind-numbing. Analyzing, questioning, seeking alternatives, and determining what makes sense is exhilarating and what education and the learning process should be. Content is retained but only after critical analysis.

Admittedly, content in the social and behavioral sciences is more open to a variety of interpretations on a broad array of theories and concepts than physical sciences, other hard sciences, history, mathematics, and so forth. However, every field has differing views, theories, and data on a wide range of concepts and "facts." Every process and tool provided in this chapter can be used in all college classrooms (K–12 in a modified manner) in some form with limited variation. It may take some tinkering, but teachers will see the value in using logical principles, providing students with similar exercises, questions, examples, and so on, when they experience the impact on students and the results.

Beyond the work in the classroom and during all formal education years, everyone can utilize these logical principles to evaluate all areas of everyday life. When reading magazines, papers, or other published mainstream material, you should be aware of potential obstacles that prevent you from making a proper judgment. Certainly, when accessing social media, internet postings, television shows, and other media it is important to step back and use these obstacles to clearing thinking tools to determine the value of the content being read or heard.

Remember these are obstacles to clear thinking because they inhibit the objective evaluation of content.

The remainder of this chapter provides the details of how critical thinking is implemented in the classroom focusing on utilization of a textbook and other materials. Although this is in an introductory psychology class, the process can be readily adapted to any course content.

THE FIRST DAY OF CLASS

This section is to provide teachers with a general format for introducing critical thinking in their classrooms. This is presented to college classes, but it can be modified to fit most grade levels in some manner. The overview of how it is introduced can be reasonably similar. It is important to begin each semester with this introduction to prepare students for what they will experience.

To set the stage for the HCE it is important to set the parameters for what it entails. This is an overview of what is presented and discussed with students during the first session each semester. Teachers should use this as a template for introducing critical thinking in their classrooms.

To introduce critical thinking to students on the first day of class, they are asked what is the purpose of formal education and specifically higher education. Every semester, students universally provide the same array of answers. Their responses are put on a white board for discussion. These include to get a better job, broaden general knowledge, and similar responses. Then a single answer is written on the white board, "to teach you how to think." Thinking requires more than information acquisition and categorizing it in the brain. It requires active processing and specific tools and techniques to help students process information and make decisions about validity and value. This is the role of the teacher, to provide the tools and guidance to assist students to think about what they read and hear with critical analysis.

At some point there will not be a teacher to sort out information for students. They will be on their own and we have failed students if we have not equipped them with at least some rudimentary tools to critically evaluate material. An essential goal of education and the teacher specifically is to prepare students for the time when they will have to think on their own, determine the correctness of information, know how to seek alternatives, and ultimately make decisions based on their analysis.

Although the Socratic Method is not specifically used in this class, the process is similar to what Socrates formulated 2,400 years ago. It is to encourage interchange between students and teachers regarding the content of the course. It minimizes lecturing and content memorization and promotes the need for critical thinking, analysis, and reaching conclusions that survive the rigors of this effort. This classroom experience emphasizes group discussions, questioning, using an expansive array of information sources, seeking alternative views and overall creating a learning environment that is student centric.

The following can be written on a white board for discussion to provide a general overview of analytical thinking. The sequencing of the Socratic Method[1] is to

1. Clarify Concepts
2. Probe Assumptions
3. Probe Rationale, Reasons, and Evidence
4. Question Viewpoints and Perspectives
5. Probe Implications and Consequences

6. Question the Question

The HCE does not focus on these in the sense of basing the critical thinking process on them. This method is given to students to make them aware that critical thinking as learning technique has existed for a long time and that process used during the semester incorporates the Socratic Method in a general manner. There is an emphasis on questioning everything, looking for logical thinking errors, and concerns about the vested interest of the person writing or espousing the information presented. This last point is very important. Students are continually asked what they think the vested interest of the writer, researcher, reviewer, among others, might be and how that could impact their perspectives. Sometimes it is as simple as who funded the research effort or the author. Often it can be more difficult, although armed with analytical skills students usually will discern the vested interest and how that could potentially impact outcomes. It is important to emphasize this does not automatically mean that what is being reported or the foundation of the research are faulty, but it provides perspective and may at least call the results into question.

Students are then told that critical thinking is important for many reasons which will be reinforced and expanded upon on during the semester, but one key point is that at some time in the future there will not be a teacher to help former students wade through content, beliefs, opposing ideas, and more. What will former students do then? Have they been equipped to make judgments without the teacher? The traditional classroom has not done this because it focuses on a narrow range of content memorization with limited time given to evaluate it.

Without formal instruction and utilization of critical thinking students are minimally equipped to evaluate and determine what makes sense or seems mostly likely correct or not. One outcome the HCE strives for is to provide students with the necessary tools for when they no longer have a teacher to determine what is important or factual. Students should be equipped to wade through ideas and opinions so that they can decide the value or lack thereof. That is what students in the HCE gain, the skills to be able to assess information, understand how to find additional content, and make decisions based on logical thinking.

This is a significant change for students, but one that will ultimately be of great benefit to them. The need is to stimulate them, create thinking, nudge them to look beyond the answers in the textbook, and ultimately change their perspective of what the classroom experience is to what it should be. Given that all students have been through years of essentially the same educational process, far different than what they are going to experience within this classroom format, gaining their buy-in to this is essential.

This is why the content provided in the first class must be an overview of the semester in a manner that engages students without overwhelming them. The three documents noted in chapter 5 are discussed. In particular, the *Obstacles to Clear Thinking* are reviewed and discussed in detail. This is the foundational document for all class activity and it is important for students to grasp the intent of each obstacle and understand the value of understanding how to use them.

The HCE is a combination of critical analysis, utilization of logical principles, research, activities that emphasize and promote thinking, and discourse among everyone in the class. There is not an emphasis on memorization, reliance on one source (such as a textbook), an assumption that the teacher has all (most) of the answers, or a reliance on content tests as the focus for determining student growth.

The learning for all students progresses because of the collective enthusiasm for these discussions and the fact that they are given sanction to disagree and provide their own analysis or thoughts. They are told to not be wedded to the textbook or what a limited number of experts think. They are encouraged to do the thinking. They are an integral part of their learning process. The teacher is the facilitator and guide, not the controller of the information flow.

They leave each class period thinking, yet armed with content that is accepted based on discussion and evaluation. Every discussion ends with lists on the white board of why something is of value, what questions there may be, what seems to make the most sense.

The materials presented below are revised periodically, new materials added, and some modified or eliminated. To keep the class fresh and current it is always necessary to bring in current content to analyze. However, the foundation pieces and techniques remain the same. It is important to emphasize that these exercises, processes, and activities can be implemented regardless of the specific course content. Everything needs the bright light of critical analysis.

THE ASSIGNMENTS

What follows are the specific assignments given to students, materials used, and methods to assess student critical thinking growth.

Textbook Analysis

The process of textbook analysis is to read the textbook utilizing the logical principles and other analytical concepts provided.

Content is discussed, but always with a focus on critical analysis, questioning research techniques, biases, opinions offered, and seeking alternatives. Some assignments ask students to locate specific obstacles to clear thinking in each chapter. Textbook analysis helps students determine value and usability and recognize issues and potential fallacies. This is done with other information as well. Teachers are encouraging students to be analytical in terms of utility, but also to not accept content merely because it is in a textbook or any other scholarly publication or source.

The following provides examples of exercises used for each chapter along with other discussion points. All of these exercises can be readily adapted to any course content at any level of high school and college (and in a modified manner in elementary and middle school). Teachers can easily find paragraphs and studies that can be analyzed and compared with other perspectives on the same issue whether in economics, mathematic, history, geography, literature, physics, chemistry, and any other course content. The main need is for teachers to undertake the effort to challenge themselves and their students to read content differently and change how they lecture or just present content. It is challenging to begin the process, but in this book (this section in particular) the reader is being provided with the process, structure, and actions needed to implement critical thinking in any classroom. The initial need to create a structure is done for you; just replicate and refine it to fit a particular course or class content. Parents and others can participate in this effort if teachers provide them with insights regarding what is expected from students in high school and perhaps earlier.

These are the instructions given to students for chapter analysis: use these examples as the format for how you should respond to the two questions assigned to you for each chapter. These examples show how to analyze the paragraph(s) in the odd numbered chapters (essentially what can be done with the information and any concerns) and in the even numbered chapters how to use and present the obstacles to clear thinking via close analysis of the content. There work is then discussed in small groups during class time.

Here is an example of how students are to respond to assigned paragraphs in the textbook. Typically, multiple paragraphs are selected and assigned randomly to students. This example deals with the importance of social linking. The paragraphs in the textbook explained the value of social linking in all aspects of life. Students are asked what can be done with this information regarding the notion that strong social links enhance health and longevity. Secondly, they are to ask questions regarding how the information could have been gathered and the outcomes proven. Essentially, the utility and value of the information, tempered by questioning the research process and outcomes.

These are the teacher's comments after students read the assigned book section:

If correct, based on the evidence from several studies, it appears that everyone should maintain frequent social interaction and a network of acquaintances to bolster our long-term health and longevity. This is of particular importance in balancing our family interactions and having close relationships with others. Since social support networks lead to healthier behaviors (nutrition, exercise, fewer "bad" habits, deal better with stress, improved self-esteem, etc.) it makes sense to ensure children establish these early on. This also raises the issue of children isolating others in schools, on the playground, and in other situations. Educators and parents need to be aware of this isolation in the school. Perhaps classes or other presentations on the importance of social links and how to help one another to be more connected in school should be provided.

Efforts should be increased for students to spend time with the elderly (including parents and grandparents) and should encourage them to get involved in social activities that engage others in meaningful relationships. Personally, everyone should make sure that we develop and maintain close relationships with a variety of people to ensure short- and long-term physical and mental health.

Some questions that might be asked are these: Does it matter if the links are not always positive? What difficulties could there be for the researchers reaching these conclusions? How could their conclusions be proven? How could they gather such information and if self-report, is it accurate? Are there differences by age, gender, or other demographics? *(End of teacher's analysis of the paragraphs.)*

Using this as an example, for odd numbered chapters students are assigned a paragraph(s) and asked how the information can be used and what issues there are with the content and conclusions.

There are two assignments for even numbered chapters. For the first even numbered chapter and every other even number chapter thereafter, several paragraphs are selected and randomly assigned to students to be discussed in small group discussion after completion. This was a different assignment than for odd numbered chapters. For these chapters students are tasked with using the obstacles to clear thinking in the manner noted below.

Here is an example using a paragraph from the textbook with the letters designating the teacher's analysis: the letters note the obstacles to clear thinking and are explained after the paragraph.

"To these facts we can add one more: the dramatic increase in anxiety levels noted earlier is also true of depression. With each new generation, the rate of depression is increasing. What is more, the disorder is striking earlier (now often in the late teens). This is true not only in Canada and the United States but also in Germany, Italy, France, Lebanon, New Zealand, Taiwan, and Puerto Rico (Cross-National Collaborative Group, 1992). In Australia,

12 percent of adolescents interviewed reported symptoms of depression. Most hid it from parents; almost 90 percent of their parents perceived their depressed teen as not suffering from depression."

Obstacles to clear thinking in paragraph:

A. Begging the question: "To these facts we can add one more." This is begging the question because it assumes the prior statements are proven and there is general agreement on these prior "facts." They have accepted them as true and given that add one more. First prove them to be true before using them to build upon. However, in the "normal" classroom this would be accepted as fact and we are now adding another fact. Students should remember these facts and will be tested on them.
B. Emotional term/value judgment: "dramatic increase." What makes it dramatic? Term is meant to influence the reader's thinking. Is it more so than expected or might it be within a normal range? Is it important that it is dramatic?
C. Non sequitur: "With each new generation . . ." This overlooks factors such as the variance in diagnostic abilities now and in the past, and the more openness that exists in today's world to reveal depression. Numbers may be higher because we are better at assessing depression or individuals are more open to acknowledging they are depressed and willing to seek help. Also seems to imply that this is a continuing ever-increasing phenomenon. Are there peaks and valleys or has it always been on the incline continuously?
D. Begging the question: "This is not only true in . . ." They are accepting that the data in Canada and the U.S. is correct and therefore we can universally gather statistics in a similar, and they think, valid manner. Most importantly it assumes the data is correct in America and it is also true in Canada. This is certainly questionable.
E. Self-report issues: "Teens reporting depressive symptoms" accurately which is questionable. Teens often have difficulty assessing their expressive behavior or why they feel the way they do. All self-report results must be questioned based on other factors that could vary the content of their statements. Observation is helpful, although observer bias then becomes a factor.
F. Non sequitur: "Most hid it from parents . . ." Therefore, the parents never knew? If they were depressed were there never any obvious symptoms? Some behaviors are difficult to conceal and depression is among them. It is a physical as well as emotionally debilitating concern and although teens may try to hide it, if they are depressive there will be indicators.

G. Begging the question: "almost 90 percent of parents"—This assumes that the teens are reporting accurately to the researchers (they are making assumptions about the parents based on teen perceptions, which seems to be questionable). Accuracy of information cannot be assumed to be true when there can be reporting issues and diagnostic errors.

Value of this paragraph: If the information in this is true, we need to be more watchful of teens, perhaps developing and refining diagnostic tools to determine potential for depression earlier on than we do. Also there should be some training and/or general training for parents to determine behavior issues with teens, especially depression.

However, with the critical analysis, students understand there are many questions about the content and conclusions, and therefore more research may be of value to determine whether or not the general content is accurate and generalizable.

Starting with chapter 4 and then every other even numbered chapter students are to find three obstacles to clear thinking in the book rather than the teacher providing them with paragraphs. They are to note the page, provide the content, and then the assessment.

Examples:

Value judgment/appeal to emotion: Page 345: Relying solely on these tests to make critical decisions affecting individual lives is not warranted and possibly even unethical.—This is her opinion and not necessarily agreed upon by everyone. She is value judging testing. Also, begs the question that we are doing this. This needs to be proven that some are relying on tests before a case can be built to question it.

Post hoc fallacy: Page 507: Because of the archetypal patterns in the collective unconscious, we perceive and react in certain predictable ways. — Assumes first of all that we can identify distinct patterns and then that these patterns create predictable behavior when it could be other variables such as learned responses. Also, they always create the same behavior, or are there other factors that might intervene?

Begging the question: Page 242: Punishment plays a significant and unavoidable role in our society.—Assumes that punishment is unavoidable when it may be avoidable in many situations. Also depends upon how punishment is defined. Additionally, what does significant mean? In comparison to other factors? Does it matter what the punishment is or what caused the supposed need for punishment?

After the analysis time is given to discussing how to use this information, if it is valid, and what additional information might be of value before making a judgment about its validity and utility.

Initially this is a bit of a struggle for students, but as the semester moves along, they become more proficient and find the process intellectually invigorating. It is a different way to read and after improving their critical thinking skills it becomes easier and "fun" in addition to being an invaluable assessment tool.

Literature Review

Articles are sourced from journals, magazines, newspapers, and other print media because students and all citizens are bombarded with information that requires critical thinking to determine value. All materials are related to the content in an introductory psychology class based on the textbook. This is of special concern when scientific and general professional information is provided in nonprofessional magazines, newspapers, and visual media wherein information is often slanted or lacks research support. Newsstand publications are printed to sell while professional journals uphold professional standards. However, even professional journal articles are subject to analysis and potentially contain faulty or biased conclusions, which students readily find during the semester.

Every week students are given a short article to read and evaluate using the obstacles to clear thinking. The purpose of doing this is to move them away from just reading and noting the high points. Not just accepting or not accepting content based on their personal biases or general beliefs or what they think the teacher's perspective is. The focus is to get them to read articles or any material and judge whether or not it has sufficient validity to be accepted or if there is a need for more research. These articles are on a wide range of topics with a psychological bent. Teachers in every field can readily do the same thing. Some of the article titles or subject matter are on violence, women being socially and economically successful, the value of self-help books, media, should we forcibly prevent suicide, the impact of gender roles and more. They are to read them and then provide an analysis. A white board is used to collect their ideas for additional discussion and narrowing.

The article is then discussed in more detail, and the teacher provides additional insights and questions. This is not to reject the article, but rather to open student thinking to read more closely and evaluate everything they read. Students are given time during class to read the article and then it is discussed in terms of its value based on critical thinking and other analytical assessments. As the semester moves along it is quite satisfying to hear how well students can evaluate the validity and value of material within a few minutes.

Clearly this exercise can be done in any classroom regardless of the content. It could easily be done when a student enters fifth grade and thereafter, but also in a modified manner at any grade level.

Expanding on some of the concepts in the Obstacles to Clear Thinking handout, students are encouraged to use these evaluative points as focal points to assess the content of the material they are reviewing.

1. *Identify Inherent Biases and Assumptions*: This does not mean that statements that have bias are necessarily wrong, but it alerts the reader to the possibility. Be aware of vested interests in positions taken or statements made by others (how does the position benefit them). Look for potential biases as they present their ideas.
2. *Separate Facts from Opinions*: Too often information presented relies on one or two personal experiences rather than scientific data (especially in psychology). Look for how well they provide valid evidence for the positions presented. Is there documented evidence. Are the sources likely to have sufficient expertise to offer opinions or minimally provide views from other experts?
3. *Logical Inferences*: This highlights the need to evaluate the logic in the presentation. Look for whether or not there are inconsistencies in the overall presentation (conclusions or ideas do not logically follow).
4. *Examine Evidence*: It is important to look at diverse sources of information before determining a conclusion. By doing this, the best answer or answers can more readily be found. Look for whether or not the article has relied on only one piece of information to draw conclusions. Simple explanations are often appealing, but often too simplistic to be correct. This can arise because the research effort is narrow and fails to include or recognize information that could alter or impact the results. More often, complex causation is involved rather than a simple one-dimensional idea. Look beyond the obvious and seek alternatives. This is difficult since most of our education emphasizes one answer as do articles in mainstream media. Look for other explanations for a conclusion or develop them yourself.

Example of an Article Assesment

Here are two paragraphs from an article to show how literature reviews are conducted during the class.

"Poll: 79 Percent of Viewers Link TV Shows to Violence"

Chapter 6

With the focus on violence in the media, and a recent conference on media violence, a survey commissioned by the Family Channel may add grist to the critics' mill and give executives further cause for alarm.

According to the poll, conducted by the Gallup Organization among 1,015 adults aged 18 and over, 79 percent of viewers are convinced that TV shows either "strongly contribute" or "somewhat contribute" to violence in general. In addition, 86 percent said TV violence "strongly contributes" or "somewhat contributes" to violence among children under 18. Not surprisingly, younger viewers were less troubled by violence than older viewers. By a 2 to 1 majority those interviewed believe that television depicts negative values more than positive ones.

If this class did not focus on critical thinking but rather just discussion of the information the content would be viewed as something worth retaining. Perhaps questions could appear on a test regarding articles read in class. Students might be required to memorize some of the data and remember the outcomes cited. Rather than questioning or determining why the information is of value, in most classrooms it would merely be discussed in terms of how it can be used.

Analysis and discussion in the HCE:

Title: Poll: 79 percent of viewers link TV shows to violence. (A) *So what? What do viewers know about the link of TV to violence? Begging the question that there is evidence that it does exist.*

"With the focus on violence in the media, and a recent conference on media violence, a survey was commissioned by the Family Channel." (B) *Vested interest in the outcome. The results are suspect based on who is paying to have the survey done.* "May add grist to the critics' mill and give executives further cause for alarm." (C) *Begging the question. Assumes that executives are already alarmed and now they should be more so. No evidence this is true.*

"According to the poll, conducted by the Gallup Organization among 1,015 adults aged 18 and over." (D) *Small sample size amounting to less than 200 per decade of age and need information on demographics.* "Seventy-nine percent of viewers are convinced." (E) *What does convinced mean, that* TV shows either "strongly contribute" or "somewhat contribute" to violence in general? (F) *How are all three of these concepts defined and what do they mean to the respondents?* In addition 86 percent said TV violence "strongly contributes" or "somewhat contributes" to violence among children under 18. (G) *Based on what information and in what ways? Not surprisingly,* (H) *why not? Based on what? Likely begging the question because it assumes this to be so based on some unknown and perhaps unproven viewpoints.* "Younger viewers were less troubled." (I) *Over simplification of a complex issue and how is this defined.* "By violence than older viewers. By a 2 to 1 majority those interviewed believe that television depicts negative values more than positive ones." (J) *How are these defined, and do we all agree on how they are categorized and which ones specifically?*

The remainder of the two-page article is reviewed in the same manner. After completing the analysis there is a discussion regarding the value and lack of value and how it could be used or not used. Here is a brief example for the above excerpt:

If the research is correct parents should be vigilant regarding television shows watched by their children. They should be more present to explain what is happening and that it is not an example of acceptable behavior. Other comments can be offered by parents and other adults to provide a counterbalance to what is being viewed.

If the research is not accurate as determined by the numerous obstacles to clear thinking, then more research is needed that is funded by organizations without a vested interest in the outcome. Even if there is some validity, the fact that it was funded by the Family Channel raises questions. The conclusion they want readers to reach is that all of the other channels show violence, but the Family Channel doesn't, so watch the Family Channel.

Other points can be made pro and con for this piece of research, but these should suffice to provide an example of how part of the critical analysis is done.

Often just the titles of articles slant the readers' perspective before knowing the content; they are designed to influence the reader before reading the article. The titles are designed to cause the reader to prejudge the content. A journalist acquaintance noted that with digital versions of a paper they may change a title several times if there are not enough clicks. The title attracts readers, and it must be provocative enough to ensure expansive readership. Often, much of the content does not substantiate the title, but they achieved their goal: expand the number of clicks to ensure advertisers that readership is high. It is much the same with many titles of professional articles; the title must attract readers. This does not mean the content is automatically problematic, but it should cause readers to be vigilant. To highlight this concern, here are examples of other literature pieces that the class evaluated. The titles influence the reader to accept the content in the manner presented. It can diminish the ability of the reader to evaluate the information because the title assumes that the content is accurate and irrefutable. When the articles are read and critically analyzed, students found that this may not be the case.

- Stop Pampering Gifted Children (Assumes parents are doing this. Many may be challenging them or have high expectations for performance.)

- Postpartum Depression Linked with Preteen Violence (Seems to be overstated and absolute in declaring a linkage. Or, if not doing so, what does linked mean? A correlation, a causative factor, or coincidental?)
- Scientists Find Public Is Often Misled by Faulty Research Data (How does this occur? Is it intentional or is it just a byproduct based on lack of ability to evaluate it? Who determines it is faulty? Is it the public's inability to evaluate it or is the research presented in such a manner that it is difficult for the public to determine validity? How often is "often"? Is it significant?)
- Teen Depression Can Affect Adult Happiness (This would require a fairly long-term longitudinal study. It also requires the ability to accurately diagnose depression and determine what constitutes happiness, which is not readily determinable. Self-report and observer bias can also impact outcomes.)
- Blame Your Peers, Not Your Parents (Assumes children blame their parents. Exactly for what are they blaming their parents? Why are peers more likely to be the blame? Does the blame differ based on what the issues or actions are before blame is assigned?)

Small Group Discussions

Small group learning and discussion is an excellent way to engage students in assessing material and collectively evaluating their thinking on an issue. In the HCE, small groups are regularly used to discuss one topic or giving different topics to each small group. The purpose is to have the groups generate ideas regarding different ways to look at a research result, a theory, a treatment technique, or a host of other subject matter.

Topics include a piece of research cited in the textbook, something that is happening in the world at the moment that relates to psychology or having students generate ideas on issues such as how to treat a specific psychological problem, how to modify behavior, what they think motivates a person to do a mass shooting, perspectives on preventing suicides, and many other topics. They are psychological in nature but can readily be related to everyday experiences or occurrences.

The topics relate to chapter content but are designed to have students generate additional ideas. They are given five minutes to individually write ideas for the question, issue, or topic and then have a group discussion. To encourage full participation, one student is the note taker for the group and then each student gives one idea. This continues around the group until all ideas are given. The teacher circulates to each group to hear what they are discussing and help with critical analysis suggestions.

Then the group discusses the ideas and determines which seem best. They also offer critical analysis techniques in terms of asking questions about their discussion points. It may be simple things such as pointing out some obstacles to clear thinking or asking other questions. After fifteen to twenty minutes the discussions stop and the results are presented to the entire class. The same procedure is used. Each group has a spokesperson provide one of their ideas and this continues until all ideas are given. Obviously, the groups will have some of the same responses. Only those not already listed on the white board are offered as each group provides their responses. After this is completed, a discussion ensues including critical analysis and a summary of what makes the most sense is determined. The teacher guides this discussion and may add in some thoughts that were not offered by the students.

These group discussions provide multiple learning experiences including individual thoughts, group discussion and refinement, critical analysis, and summary points that bring the content together.

Group Assignments

Additionally, specific assignments are given to students to research and then discuss in class. Students conduct research on topics selected by the teacher related to various chapter content to expand their knowledge beyond the textbook. All students are assigned to one of the topics during the semester. This is designed to expose them to other well-researched positions and ideas, some of which may contradict or support the content in the book.

As with every other activity provided, group assignments can be readily adapted to other course content. The focus is on topics that either have a pro/con option or comparison of differing theories, ideas of treatment, diagnoses, or any topic that is relevant to the course work.

The purpose of these assignments is to motivate students to read other resources in addition to the textbook. Typically, there are two to four students in each group. Students are expected to find different perspectives, pros and cons, and other comparisons.

Students are encouraged to bring in books or other materials and read from them or provide excerpts. Information is much more readily available on the internet and much of what they found was sourced from there. However, students are encouraged to make some use of libraries because it is a different experience and provides different opportunities to locate information. The resources used must be provided.

Examples of Group Topics:

Group One: Psycho-Dynamic/Psychoanalytic and Behavioral Theories
Group Two: Cognitive and Humanism Theories

Group Three: Neuro-Psychology (Neuro-Science) and Evolutionary Psychology Theories
Group Four: Sociocultural and Social Learning Theories
Group Five: Varying Perspectives on Employee Motivation and Performance
Group Six: Pros and Cons of Mental Hospital Commitment
Group Seven: The Positive and Negative Impact of Media on Behavior
Group Eight: The Psychological Impact of Stereotypes, Prejudice, and Bias

For these assignments and most other classroom discussions, students and the teacher sit in a large circle or horseshoe to ensure discussion is more interactive, allowing everyone to participate. The teacher participates, but usually to clarify, ask questions, and occasionally add information to expand the content the students are providing. The teacher serves as a scribe, writing key points on a white board. At the end of each of these discussions, the summary information on the white board is discussed, questioned, and information added by the teacher or students. Students have content, but it is presented in a different manner and the outcome for every discussion varies from semester to semester based on the information students locate and present to the class. There is a core of information that is generally similar, but since these topics are expansive, different material is usually found each semester.

MEASURING STUDENT CRITICAL THINKING GROWTH

The assignments during the semester provide students with preparation for measuring their critical thinking growth. None of the weekly assignments are graded. They are used to understand how to think critically while reading the textbook and other material. The mid-term assignments and final research paper comprise the student's assessment and their grade for the class.

Rather than testing for content memorization, these assignments emphasize growth in critical analysis. The purpose of measurement assignments is to provide students with opportunities to indicate their developing analytical skills in a variety of ways. Grading is primarily based on the student's ability to utilize critical thinking. Although this may seem subjective, to some degree all testing is subjective based on what a teacher or a source test bank decides is important to know.

Mid-term Assignments

Using what they have learned and used during the first several weeks of the semester, students are given assignments to gauge their critical thinking growth.

1. Questions focused on analyzing book content
2. Locating examples of selected obstacles to clearing thinking in the book.
3. Discerning similarities and differences in multiple definitions of psychological terms

Part One:

For each question you are assigned (either 1 or 2) use the book to access the information needed for background to answer the question and then provide your insights and thoughts based on your reading and analysis of the information. You are to provide a written response to question 1 or question 2 based on your assigned group and everyone must provide a written response to question 3. Do not repeat the information provided in the book. The intent of these questions is for you to think about and utilize the book's information to formulate your answers. Provide more than a few sentences to respond to the questions which require your thinking and analysis. Do not do any other research for this; just use the book as a resource to develop your responses. *Use separate paper to respond to these questions and those in part two below.*

1. What questions and concerns do you have regarding twin studies as a basis for determining nature versus nurture influences? Do you think that physiology defines who we are (why or why not—defend views)?
2. Provide your ideas and reasons for your position regarding whether gender behavioral differences are principally caused by genetics or environment. That is, which do you think is more influential and why do you think so (defend your views)? Everyone responds to this question:
3. Which do you think is most influential in determining how we interact and what we think/believe, parents or peers? Defend why you think so.

Part Two:

Evaluating sections of the textbook and having a wide range of issues found by the students was quite enlightening for them. It taught them how to read differently.

Using the descriptions in the Obstacles to Clear Thinking handout locate one example of each of these two key obstacles, plus one more of your choice. *Provide the complete example with the page number it is located on in the book and respond to the request for substantiation.*

1. Post Hoc Fallacy (Causal Relationship Issue): (also provide what other variables could have caused the result stated).
2. Value Judgment/Appeal to Emotion: (also provide why you think this is so).
3. Find ONE of any of the other Obstacles to Clear Thinking and defend why you think it is.

Rather than just accepting information students now are evaluating it in terms of its logical conclusion or other obstacles that may impact its value. It is understood that they will accept some of the views and not others.

Part Three:

Students are asked to compare multiple definitions of the same word. Even terms that seem to have some universal components are defined slightly differently or the emphasis in the definition is different. Therefore, if the only definition offered is in the textbook, how do students and others know if it is the best definition, provides a complete view of the term, or should be combined with other definitions, and so forth? Since analysis is the key part of this assignment it is better for the teacher to find the definitions for each term and have students do the analysis.

Students are provided with a term used in psychology that has many varied definitions (which is essentially any term) even though the textbook only provides one as though it is the only one. The teacher provides six to eight terms with multiple definitions of each, and students are to compare them. Each student only gets one term. When they complete the take home exam, they sit in small groups to discuss the terms (each student in each group has a different term).

This type of learning exercise can readily be used in any course content such as interpretation of literature, defining terms or analyzing theories in physical sciences, or evaluating mathematical word problems, equations, or concepts. The social and behavioral sciences may seem easier because of the fluidity of defining concepts, but every field of study has differing views of key concepts, theories, and expert opinions. All certainly have ways to ask students to solve an issue or problem.

No field of study is immune from disagreements regarding some fundamental data or information. Yes, there is a range of information in all fields that is highly probable and some almost universally accepted, but even some of this is open to interpretation. The role of the teacher is to provide students with the tools to evaluate information, opinions, and outcomes, and give them the opportunity to make judgments with guidance. A foundation can be provided, but then the learning process should be expanded to encourage thinking and analysis. This is what these assignments are about, looking at definitions of the same term and noting how they are different or similar and determining which one the student can defend as the best or most logical.

Example: Comparing Definitions of Stress

To indicate to students that there are numerous definitions of even the most common psychological terms, as part of the mid-term exam they are given six definitions of a term and asked to analyze them.

Five terms are selected by the teacher and six definitions from various sources located for each. These are then randomly given to students. When they complete their analysis by the assigned date, they are put in groups with the five different words and discuss them. In this way they are able to hear about several terms other than the one they worked on. They then discuss them as a group and decide which definition they think is best and worst which many times differs from the person completing work on the term.

Directions for this part of the exam: As part of the mid-term examination, you are to compare and contrast one key psychological term which will provide clarity regarding why it is important to read critically and to seek multiple sources to gain insight into differences before deciding what makes sense to you. Relying on only one source, such as the textbook, will provide only one definition or perspective which may not be the best one and only indicative of one person's view.

Numerous terms are offered in psychology textbooks as though there is a uniform definition agreed upon by everyone in the field. However, this is often not the case. This exercise is designed to reveal that there are differences in how "experts" define even basic terms in psychology. Of course, this is also true when reading any material regardless of the source.

This exercise provides students with the opportunity to evaluate for themselves the varying definitions of common terms in psychology. This is not an exhaustive list, there numerous others.

1. Compare them in terms of how they differ from one another. For example, one definition states this and the others don't, or definitions two and four state this and others don't and numerous other comparisons.
2. Choose the definition you think is best and defend why you think so.

3. Choose the definition you think is the worst and defend why you thinks so.

Examples of how to do this analysis

Definitions of Stress:

1. Stress is a condition or feeling experience when a person perceives that demands exceed the personal and social resources the individual is able to mobilize.
2. Stress is forces from the outside world impinging on the individual and is a normal part of life that can help us learn and grow. Conversely, stress can cause significant problems.
3. Stress arises when individuals perceive that they cannot adequately cope with the demands being made on them or with threats to their well-being.
4. Stress can only be sensibly defined as a perceptual phenomenon arising from a comparison between the demand on the person and their ability to cope. An imbalance in this mechanism, when coping is important, gives rise to the experience of stress and to the stress response.
5. Stress results from an imbalance between demands and resources. Stress is the psychological, physiological, and behavioral response by an individual when they perceive a lack of equilibrium between the demands placed upon them and their ability to meet those demands, which, over a period of time leads to ill-health.
6. Stress is any force that pushes a psychological or physical function beyond its range of stability, producing stress within the individual.

Analysis of Differences: This analysis is brief for purposes of this book, but it gives the clear indication that these definitions are not the same and also have questionable premises and conclusions. Providing distinctive differences.

1. States that stress occurs when demands exceed resources to cope. What sort of resources internal, external, physical, or mental or other resources? Does it matter what sort of demands?
2. States that stress is a normal part of life. What does this mean exactly? Why should it be, is it not possible to cope universally or at least experience limited anxiety that is not debilitating?
3. States that stress occurs where there are threats to well-being. What does this mean, physical, psychological, life experiences? Define well-being. Too broad.

4. States that their definition is the only sensible way to define stress which is as a perceptual phenomenon. So, it is perception and not necessarily actual. Also states that it occurs when coping is important. This is minimally an appeal to authority and a non sequitur. It seems to focus on what one perceives as an issue rather than one that actually may occur.
5. States that it is a psychological, physiological, and behavioral response to demands and can lead to ill health. This one seems all encompassing and the only one that mentions ill health potential.
6. States that stress occurs when any force pushes a psychological or physical force that causes instability. Seems vague and overly broad.

Although there are similarities in all of the definitions, there are variables among all of them with slightly different emphasis.

Best: Definition 2 seems to provide sufficient focus while allowing for the breadth of possibilities for impact.

Worst: Definition 4, although expansive seems to include some points that muddy the definition such as when coping is important and calling it a perceptual phenomenon.

Before the completed papers are given to the teacher part of the class time is spent in small groups wherein students discuss their responses to the questions to gain different perspectives. The teacher circulates among the groups to listen to interchanges and offer insights.

Final Assignment: Research Paper

There is a research paper due at the end of the semester wherein students select a topic of interest to them. To assist in the process, they are provided with a list of twenty or more topics to select from. They can choose any topic of interest (approved by the teacher) or select one from the list. These are brief papers, approximately seven to ten pages, although some students do more. Twice during the semester there are quick reviews of how students are doing with their research and assistance provided if needed.

This research effort offers students the opportunity to get deeper into a topic and find material that reveals differences. As with all components of the class students are expected to point out examples of obstacles to clear thinking in their research findings. Evaluation of these papers focuses on the teacher's knowledge of what is accessible on a topic, the breadth of resources located, and students' analysis of what they found.

When completed, students are placed in groups of four or five and they read and discuss their papers. In this manner students get to learn about other topics in psychology and how other students evaluated the material they found. The teacher circulates, sitting in with each group several times to listen and at times guide the discussion.

OUTCOME: STUDENTS ARE TAKING CHARGE OF THEIR LEARNING

Students initially find these assignments not only challenging, but unusual in the sense of asking them to locate relevant material, evaluate it, and make decisions regarding its importance to them. As noted earlier, one does not need to memorize material to retain it. What is valued and found important will be retained. Other information is incidental and can be recalled when specific cues trigger remembrance.

Reading and enjoying the process of learning rather than reviewing material students think will be on a test is appreciated by students based on their comments. By the mid-point of each semester, most students value not having to memorize what the teacher thinks is important or what a standardized test book determines that students should remember.

The HCE broadens the scope of what students determine they should retain. It moves them to be lifelong learners using skills and techniques that will serve them beyond any classroom, any teacher, and any degree. Books and other materials are resources, readily available, especially with internet access. Why memorize minutiae when you can readily find it? It's better to understand how to analyze the content and determine the value of it. Students leave the class armed with techniques and skills to read differently and analyze content to determine what makes sense to them. Relatively the same content is covered during the semester as in any other introductory psychology class. The main difference is how it is viewed. This is what students leave the class with and most acknowledge it.

There are some comments toward the end of this section which offer indications of students' reactions to the class and the value they place in having this opportunity. They leave the class with content, but also skills to use throughout their educational endeavors and beyond.

THE LAST DAY OF CLASS

A semester is never enough time with students, partially because of the concern that when they walk out of the room for the last time, they will move back into the educational system that focuses on memorization rather than critical thinking and on answers rather than questions. They may struggle to maintain what this class offered them. Some will persist and use critical thinking when asking questions, but many classrooms they will go on to will not foster what this class has planted, and this is disheartening.

At the end of each semester, an overview of the class is provided. A summarization of what students likely expected, what they were initially told during the first class to launch this educational experience, what outcomes they should leave with, a general overview of content and perspectives on what took place, and reflections on education in general.

Before they are presented with an overview and handouts summarizing key thoughts, this is the time to ask them what they gained from the class. What they thought initially when critical thinking was presented as the focal point for all class activities. Their perspectives on the various classroom assignments, the assessment pieces they completed and other components utilized during the semester. This is an interesting discussion, because it provides their perspective of the value of this educational experience.

They leave this class as different students than when they entered. There has been a change in how they read and what they accept as answers. They have developed critical thinking skills that will serve them well in the years ahead.

SUMMARY OF THE CLASS

(This summary is verbally presented.)

From my perspective, here are some of the key learning outcomes that you have gained. We will discuss how they align with your thinking.

1. Knowledge base of psychology (major concepts, perspectives, theories, historical trends and more).
2. Have a general understanding of research methods in psychology (understand and apply basic methods of research).
3. Awareness of the various applications of psychology (understand how psychology is used in all aspects of life).
4. Understand techniques of learning and utilizing values (weigh evidence, tolerate ambiguity, and act ethically).
5. Learned new skills or expanded on current intellectual and practical skills including critical thinking, inquiry, analysis, written and oral communication, information literacy, and problem solving.
6. Developed increased awareness of personal and social responsibility including intercultural knowledge, ethical reasoning and action, foundations and skills for lifelong learning, and civic knowledge and engagement.

At the end of each semester, students are given three documents to reflect on as they exit the class and move on in their education, careers, and community life. The first puts the course in perspective. This provides a summary of the key outcomes they received. The second reflects on education in general. What constitutes education in America and what we can do to change it. The third focuses on the importance and usefulness of critical thinking. These are discussed briefly during this final class to highlight their value and importance.

THE CLASS IN PERSPECTIVE

(Document number one)

This is an overview of what was discussed and accomplished in the class. If students have read the book and actively listened and participated in class, they gained a solid cross-section of psychological theory and applications. The purpose of a formal classroom education is to provide an open forum for discussion, prod students to think about what they believe, and instill in them a desire to learn and pursue knowledge. Students were provided with an array of learning techniques and discussion topics. The principal teaching strategies and activities during this semester were these:

1. Used critical thinking as the focus throughout the class and encouraged students to be open-minded.
2. Provided research techniques to substantiate psychological concepts, theories, and opinions.
3. Reviewed and discussed ten major psychological theories in terms of their underpinnings, research base, differences from one another, and value.
4. Overviews of applications of psychological concepts. Utilizing numerous theories and treatment techniques lead to discussions of applications in various settings including mental hospital commitment, treatment of numerous psychological concerns, employee motivation and performance, causes and impacts of bias and prejudice, media impact on behavior.
5. Used small group discussions on a wide range of topics; outcomes are discussed with the entire class. Some of these included psychological obstacles for success for women through various stages of life, psychological value and impact of self-help books, psychological impact of gender roles, treatment outcome research, delinquent gang behavior and values, and numerous other topics. Incorporated in these

discussions were the use of logical thinking concepts to question or affirm various views.
6. Pertinent articles were provided for discussion and evaluation. Some of these topics included peer versus parental impact on children, violence in the media producing violence in viewers and readers, research on attention deficit disorder, value, and concerns with gifted student programs.
7. Read the book differently than students have experienced in other classrooms. Discussed material in the book and questioned some of its validity and sought other resources for additional information on key concepts.

Ultimately students leave a basic introductory psychology class taught with the HCE approach with a broad sense of the many varied theories in psychology, the sometimes contradictory views of experts, a sense of the different applications of psychology in treatment and everyday life, an ability to read differently with an emphasis on validity, and most importantly a value and excitement for this critical thinking process and learning in general.

REFLECTIONS ON EDUCATION

(Document Number Two)

As you know the philosophy of education in this classroom is to encourage students to think for themselves and to begin (or enhance) the process of how to determine what has value and what is questionable. That is, critical thinking and independent judgments rather than rote memorization.

Jerry Farber views the educational process as molding students to conform to the routine of memorization and test taking.[2] How can this mold be broken? What should teachers do? Break the mold by offering students an opportunity to have discussions that not only convey "facts and conclusions," but also provide for opposing views and questioning what may be thought are the "answers" (or one book or one teacher thinks are the answers). It is done by evaluating opinions and "facts" rather than memorizing information that is arguable now and may not be factual in the future, in order to pass a test.

Books are resources. What students need to know is where to find information and how to evaluate and use what they find, rather than memorize minutiae. What is important will stick with students even though they have not been forced to memorize it. Education should be an exploratory process that opens students to a wide range of ideas and opinions, without the teacher forcing them to accept their point of view or that of the textbook authors.

Break the mold by working at changing the routine of listening to lectures, memorizing book material (writing down the key "facts"), and regurgitating it on periodic tests. It is done by guiding students to question and determine for themselves what makes sense. Break down barriers by pushing students to challenge their biases and listen to opposing views. Encouraging students to present their views and defend them even if the teacher disagrees or they have no apparent foundation. It is the teacher's role (and it should be the role of all teachers at every education level) to challenge student views and to push different thinking in order to develop comfort with being challenged and challenging the thinking of others. It is the teacher's role to encourage the expression of differing viewpoints to broaden knowledge and awareness of a range of ideas. As Alfred North Whitehead stated, "your learning is useless to you till you have lost your textbooks, burnt your lecture notes, and forgotten the minutiae which you learnt by heart for examination. The function of a university is to enable you to shed details in favor of principles."[3]

Engage students in discussions that energize them to think. Provide students with an opportunity to read a textbook in a way that they have unlikely experienced before. Provide an opportunity to research a topic of interest for a brief paper. "Tests" are partially research based and require finding differing perspectives on several topics and also a variety of critical thinking activities. Encourage students to use obstacles to clear thinking (logical principles) to analyze articles and content in the book to more clearly acknowledge that even well researched topics and issues have logical flaws. Work at opening student minds to think and evaluate how/what they read and accept.

Unfortunately, students have been told to focus over their educational careers on just getting the "answers" even if they are not necessarily correct and often not the only answers. As was noted often during the semester, of course there is material that has a very high probability of being correct, but nothing is absolute. Therefore, less time was spent evaluating certain pieces of information than others. Where there are clearly varied positions then they must be examined. Where there is a strong consensus, less time is spent evaluating, but still ensure there is no faulty logic. To paraphrase another thought from Farber, "thinking can cause pain and students will do whatever possible to avoid pain."

I value teaching and how students learn. This includes a concern with the educational process. It is understood that this process of learning is difficult for students after years of conditioning to take notes, memorize information, and make check marks on a test page. There has always been a hope that a spark will be ignited in every student. A spark to want to read, to question, explore options, challenge the "facts," think independently, and determine what views to accept.

Of course, many students find sanctuary in classes that provide the soothing comfort of "answers" and multiple-choice tests. Perhaps, in the years ahead as situations arise, students leaving this class will reflect on this experience and note, "maybe Dr. Hammes was on to something after all."

Quoting Robert Hutchins, "Far more important than knowledge is the method by which it is reached . . . educational institutions must emphasize methods of analysis and independent reflection in order for students to confront the claim of ideals and values by their alternatives."[4]

This is the essence of education and the learning process espoused in this class. The hope is that all students will carry this with them as they leave the classroom at the end of each semester and use it throughout their lifetime. You are wished every success in your future educational and career endeavors.

IMPORTANCE AND USEFULNESS OF CRITICAL THINKING

(Document Number Three)

Most important for all students some final thoughts to send you off to your ongoing formal education, career direction, and role as a citizen.

Critical thinking requires everyone to be:

- Inquisitive regarding how issues are approached.
- Concerned with becoming and remaining well-informed.
- Alert to opportunities to use critical thinking skills.
- Trusting in the processes of reasoned inquiry.
- Self-confident in the ability to reason through issues and topics in general.
- Open-minded regarding views that are divergent.
- Honest with recognition of personal biases, prejudices, and stereotypes.
- Prudent in suspending, making, or altering judgments.
- Willing to reconsider and revise views where reflection suggests changes are warranted.
- Use logical principles and concepts to aid in assessing information regardless of the source and/or apparent validity.

As you leave this class and this teacher, do not leave behind the growing ability to analyze, think critically, and determine what makes sense based on these efforts.

***

COMMENTS FROM STUDENTS

After the students left the room for the last time, I would lean against the desk and ponder what I had given them, how would they use it and did I make an impact. It was always a lonely time, reflecting on the weeks together with the group and realizing I would likely never know if my efforts to redirect their thinking about learning will make a difference in their education and lives in general.

The reward for me was having students during and at the end of the semester (and sometimes even months or years later) comment to me in person, email, or by handwritten note about how much they enjoyed the class and how it opened them to thinking differently and, in some cases changed their lives.

This is not meant to be self-aggrandizing, but merely to offer what many students thought of the class and the changes it brought for them. It is more about the learning process.

Some comments/statements I recall:

- A student noted that they learned more about critical thinking in this class than they did in a critical thinking class.
- Over the years, many students commented during the semester that they have had challenging discussions with friends, spouses, and others when they started raising questions and using the fundamentals of clear thinking. Rather than just expressing differences of opinion, they were questioning comments and ideas based on logic and this made it difficult for others since they often could not defend their views.
- A student that owned a manufacturing business brought me in as a consultant to work with managers and supervisors on problem solving and employee interaction and then with employee groups.
- A student wrote a poem to me about their experience in the class (this is buried somewhere in a memorabilia box).
- Another student wrote a poem to me about how the class had changed them (same as the one above).
- Another thanked me for bringing a breath of fresh air and turning their life around and giving them a new focus.
- Many older students commented on how they wish they would have had this class at an earlier age and how different it was from the education process they remember.
- Innumerable comments focused on how the class gave them a different perspective on learning and how they will approach education going forward.

- More broadly one class petitioned the college to start a new psychology class so they could have another semester of critical thinking.
- One student wrote a lengthy note about how this changed their life and gave them confidence to take on new things. This was in response to a note from the teacher that praised her for pushing herself to excel in class and meeting the challenge:

No, Dr. Hammes, you pushed me first then I took over. From the beginning I will be totally honest and confess and say that taking your class was at first a challenge. I used to go home and download about you to my family. You are a teacher that expects nothing but the best and you challenged me in ways that I honestly thought didn't exist anymore. I have worked for fast food for the last twenty years, and for a long time felt that was what I was going to do for the rest of my life. Then I entered in your world. (You're supposed to laugh.) You taught me how to think again, you in a way jump started my brain. I haven't attended school in a long time and I am happy you were one teacher I came into contact with. With the skills you provided for me and continued to hammer into my head every week I truly feel more ready than ever to continue my education and never give up. You have inspired me enormously. I will never ever forget you. I know you informed us that this may be your last year teaching and in 43 years of being an educator I know you have come across so many students. Please know from the bottom of my heart you changed me. I could go on and about how wonderful a teacher you have been, but I won't. (You're supposed to laugh again.) I will end by saying have a wonderful and safe holiday. I look forward to seeing you in the college hallways. Thanks Again!!!!!

This was from a student who returned to college at around age forty after years away from education and saw the value for them, and what it meant to them in terms of their education and life in general.

Older students were more likely to appreciate and engage in the process and method than younger students that recently left twelve years of content memorization and testing. These younger students knew how to achieve in that system. Many initially struggled more than older students, but those that remained flourished.

As for all teachers, student comments are appreciated and add to the fulfillment of teaching.

NOTES

1. Sawyer and others, https://www.unl.edu/gradstudies/connections/socratic-questioning, 2000.

2. Jerry Farber, *The Student as N . . . er* (Los Angeles: Los Angeles Free Press, 1967), 71.

3. Alfred North Whitehead, *Science and the Modern World* (New York: Simon and Schuster, 1997), 91.

4. Robert Hutchins, *No Friendly Voice* (Chicago: University of Chicago Press, 1936), 23.

Chapter 7

What Now?

Actions to Take

> Do not judge my intelligence by the answers I give, but instead by the questions I ask.
>
> —Mark McGranaghan, director, Electric Power Institute

Often, the classroom is focused on students providing answers to questions from the teacher and they may not feel comfortable asking questions. There is limited classroom time, and all expected content must be completed in the prescribed time. This quote encapsulates the concern. Asking questions and analyzing is essential, but most of our formal education is focused on students providing answers.

The previous chapter provided detailed techniques, materials, and strategies for presenting critical thinking in the college classroom. However, it was indicated in that chapter that most of this material can be adapted from the fifth grade to twelfth grade as well and in a more modified manner to elementary and middle school students.

The main thrust of the material presented in this chapter for implementing critical thinking and logical analysis is for college and potentially high school students. However, throughout the book it has been noted in numerous places how these thinking techniques can be utilized by others involved with children from early ages through graduate school and on to careers.

This chapter brings together ideas for teachers, students, parents, boards of education, and employers involved at all levels of formal education as well as employers. It is important that all of these groups understand how to access, understand, and utilize critical-thinking skills and logical concepts to analyze information. They should know and understand the views of others, how to conduct research, look for ways to handle job issues, and a host of other life experiences which require critical thinking and analysis.

The American Philosophical Association (cited in the *Scientific American*[1]) offers tips for teaching and encouraging critical thinking. It is important to start early. Very young children might not be ready for lessons in formal logic. But they can be taught to give reasons for their conclusions and evaluate the reasons given by others. For young children the following are research-based suggestions for teaching critical thinking and scientific reasoning to preschoolers.

- *Avoid pushing dogma.* When children are told to do things in a certain way, they should be given reasons.
- *Encourage children to ask questions.* Parents and teachers should foster curiosity in children. If a rationale doesn't make sense to a child, the child should be encouraged to voice the objection or difficulty and seek clarification.
- *Ask children to consider alternative explanations and solutions.* It's nice to get the right answer. But many problems have more than one solution. When children consider multiple solutions, they will become more flexible thinkers.
- *Get children to clarify meaning.* Children should practice putting things in their own words and be encouraged to make meaningful distinctions among choices regarding things to do such as books to read, music to listen to, or how to resolve issues with others.
- *Talk about biases.* Even very young children and grade school students can understand how emotions, motives, and cravings can influence judgments and actions taken.
- *Don't confine critical thinking to purely factual or academic matters.* Encourage children to reason about ethical, moral, and everyday issues.
- *Get children to write.* Literacy is the foundation of all learning and focuses on the four interconnected components of reading, writing, speaking, and listening. Children's early writing skills begin with drawing pictures to describe their thoughts and messages. This transitions with alphabet letter knowledge to inventive spelling, to phonetic spelling, to emergent sentence structure. Writing skills are best nurtured by praising all attempts and modeling developmental skills.

As teachers know, the process of writing helps students clarify their explanations and sharpen their arguments. They can be assigned different types of writing assignments dealing with class content or issues and situations in the community or on the playground.

Adding to above perspectives, below is a list of skills that should be taught to children beginning at an early age. Studies suggest that students become remarkably better problem solvers when we teach them to:[2]

- analyze analogies and why they are or are not analogous
- create categories and classify items appropriately
- identify relevant information for a topic or issue
- construct and recognize valid deductive arguments
- understand how to test hypotheses
- recognize common reasoning fallacies
- distinguish between evidence and interpretations of evidence
- determine what is fact and what is fiction

Here are some very simple activities from Atlas Mission[3] that can be done in preschool and in the home:

Guess What I Have: With a small toy in one hand, place both hands behind your back. Ask the child to guess what is in your hand. As they make attempts to guess, give them clues until they figure it out.

Play the "Is It True?" Game: Ask a question that starts with 'Is it true that . . . .' When they answer, ask them how they know that it is true or not and then query why they know that. If possible, ask them why it might not be true.

Work in Groups: This is a good way to engage children in the give and take of problem solving. The hardest part of this activity is getting everyone's attention. Have them decide how something should be done or reasons for something happening. They will realize that there is more than one way of doing things and they are introduced to a variety of different approaches and ideas.

Find Similarities and Differences: Play a game of pointing out similarities and differences in things. Ask them to find or voice things that are similar and different at the same time such as a fork and a spoon. Both are utensils but one is for eating salad and the other for soup.

Ask "What Happened and Why": Sit down with the child/children and look at some pictures that have a story behind them and then ask the child, "What happened in this picture and why do you think so?"

TEACHERS

Students at all education levels can understand and utilize critical thinking and logical analysis. Even young students are capable of reasoning and understanding analysis if they are guided and encouraged.

Elementary and Middle School

Elementary and middle school teachers will likely need to modify some of the materials provided in the Hammes Classroom Experience. However, the basic principles of critical thinking should be the same. Ultimately, teachers should be utilizing part of their time with students to move them to think independently, think critically, and use logical concepts to evaluate information regardless of the source.

In the early years there are basic skills that must be taught: reading, writing, understanding of basic numbers and arithmetic calculations as a foundation for future learning. But even at this early stage of the formal educational process much of what is utilized at the college level can be implemented. Start with basic *obstacles to clear thinking* that you know they can understand such as emotional appeals, conclusion not necessarily following from a premise, causal relationships that may be wrong. Most of these can be modified and taught in the early stages of education.

Encourage students to compare and contrast varying content, brainstorm, accept challenges, struggle when they do not understand, and collaborate with others. Give them concepts, issues, topics, problems to utilize critical thinking and continually encourage them.

Below are some basic questions that can be asked of students that will promote critical thinking and analysis:

1. Why do you think this is correct?
2. Based on what I just told you or you just read, do you think it is correct or do you think it could be wrong? Why do you think so? Could the opposite be correct?
3. Does the conclusion seem to follow from the information provided or do you think there could be another conclusion?
4. Do you need to know more before you decide the correctness or value of the information?
5. Why do you agree with this statement?
6. Why do you not agree with this statement?
7. What value is this information to you and how can it best be used?
8. How are these two pieces of information connected?
9. What questions would you ask about this?
10. Use games, role playing, or other activities to highlight how they could interpret things differently based on how it is presented.

Even with play time or nonacademic activities young children can be taught to be evaluative. For example:

1. If there is a disagreement with another student, asking them how it could have been handled differently.
2. Asking why they or someone else did something one way and not another.
3. Asking why someone said or did something to them in terms of why do they think they did so?
4. While observing other students' actions, ask why they think the other students acted as they did. How could they have acted differently?
5. Reinforcing with them to evaluate a situation before they act and determine if there are alternative actions they could take.

During the first four years of formal education, teachers should determine which HCE tools to use perhaps with some modification. From grades five to eight most of the materials and suggestions can be readily adapted. Given teachers' expertise they should be able to adapt the HCE material to fit the class content at their grade level.

Adapt what you think is feasible and expand from that as your students become comfortable with the process. Encourage students, make it "fun," reward their effort, and recognize their persistence. Evaluate students on their reasoning ability and openness to seeking different answers, and encourage them to ask questions.

Select the *obstacles to clear thinking* you think are appropriate for the age group and the content of your class. Modify the wording and examples to fit the grade level. You can add to them as the year goes along. Explain to students why critical thinking is important and what they will gain from it.

A child in pre- or early adolescence (fifth through eighth grade) develops and uses more complex thinking.

- Begins to show use of formal logical operations in schoolwork.
- Often questions more extensively.
- Often analyzes more extensively.

Here are some additional critical-thinking suggestions for elementary and middle school education.

- *Ask questions.* Asking open-ended questions gives students in these age ranges a chance to apply what they've learned and build on prior knowledge. It also allows them to problem solve and think on their feet and boosts self-esteem by providing an opportunity for students to express themselves in front of their peers.
- *Encourage decision-making.* Since a large part of teaching critical-thinking skills revolves around applying knowledge and evaluating solutions,

elementary and middle school teachers should encourage decision-making as much as possible. This enables students to apply what they've learned to different situations, weigh the pros and cons of a variety of solutions, then decide which ideas work best.
- *Work in groups.* Group projects and discussions are another excellent way for elementary and middle school teachers to encourage critical-thinking skills. Cooperative and collaborative learning not only exposes students to the thought processes of their classmates, it expands their thinking and worldview by demonstrating that there's typically no one right way to approach a problem.
- *Incorporate different points of view.* Some of the very best critical-thinking exercises for elementary and middle school students involve exploring a concept from multiple perspectives. This tactic not only establishes that an idea should be assessed from different points of view before an opinion is formed, but it gives students a chance to share their viewpoints while listening to and learning from others.
- *Connect different ideas.* Connecting different ideas is key to teaching critical thinking. For example, elementary school teachers can ask students if they know anyone who has to take a bus to work, and if so, why it would be important for that person to also have a train schedule or know about other transportation options. Questions like these help children consider different situations (delayed buses, schedule changes, for example) and potential solutions (taking the train instead), helping them apply prior knowledge to new contexts. Higher order questions can be asked of middle school students.
- *Inspire creativity.* Imagination is key to teaching critical thinking in elementary school and develops even more in middle school. Teachers should seek out new ways for students to use information to create something new. Art projects are an excellent way to do this. Students can also construct a different way to do something by writing a story or poem, creating a game, singing a song.
- *Brainstorm.* A time-honored tradition in elementary and middle school education, this is an excellent learning tool. It's also an excellent critical-thinking exercise, especially when paired with visual elements that bring original thinking and classroom discussions to life.[4]

As previously stated, there are basic skills that must be taught and honed, but a significant part of the early learning experience should be focused on critical thinking not thwarting this ability by over focusing on memorization and limited content. It may challenge you as a teacher, but it will be rewarding as your students become excited by the opportunity to explore and question.

High School

As students enter high school, they expand their ability to think abstractly, and their analytical skills become more expansive during the teenage years. At age thirteen, they can analyze sophisticated issues and problems and should be encouraged to do so. Teachers should assume that the student can be analytical and open to ambiguity and problem solving. Students should be given encouragement and techniques to do so. In this regard, during the high school years teachers can implement most, if not all, of the assignments, test models, discussion activities, and other components of the HCE. During these remaining developmental years, there are core pieces of information that all students should be exposed to, but even these can be critically analyzed. Often this will lead to the conclusion that the basic information offered is the best available, but minimally much of it should be assessed and optional perspectives sought.

The hope is that high school teachers will recognize the value of critical thinking and implement the parts of the HCE that fit with the curriculum emphasis and desired outcomes. We want all students to graduate at every grade level with core information and they will have it especially when critical analysis is a key part of the educational process.

From the "Education Corner, Critical Thinking Guide" a child in mid- to late adolescence (ninth through twelfth grade):

- Uses systematic thinking and begins to influence relationships with others.
- Has increased thoughts about more global concepts, such as justice, history, politics, and patriotism.
- Becomes more open to debate and develops tolerance for opposing views.
- Begins to focus thinking on making career decisions.
- Begins to focus thinking on their emerging role in adult society.[5]

How do high school teachers assist in this process? Most of what is contained in the HCE will help high school teachers guide students to think critically and analyze problems and situations in everyday life. They can assist students to develop these skills by doing role playing in the classroom or proposing situations and asking students to analyze them and determine what to do to achieve the best outcome. Critical thinking is the overarching process in all situations. High school teachers should note that the seven guiding principles in the following section on college teaching can be implemented in their classrooms as well.

College

If you are teaching college courses, the material provided in the HCE (chapter 6) can be readily adapted and applied to whatever subject matter you teach.

Below are principles of excellence and learning outcomes developed by members of the American Psychological Association Education Directorate. Essentially these are the principles that college teachers should focus on in their teaching and what students should expect as outcomes of the educational process.[6]

Here are some guiding principles that can overlay all college teaching. These principles are adaptable during the high school years as well.

> Principle One: Aim high, expect excellence.
> Principle Two: Provide guidance.
> Principle Three: Teach the art of inquiry.
> Principle Four: Engage in big questions.
> Principle Five: Prepare students for citizenship.
> Principle Six: Foster intercultural and ethical learning.
> Principle Seven: Encourage application of learning to complex problems.

These should not be isolated to specific course content, but rather woven intimately into all instruction regardless of the content.

BUILDING ADMINISTATORS

Building administrators have important roles in reinforcing positive student outcomes in the classroom. Specific to the HCE classroom, administrators can promote critical-thinking skills in the classroom through professional development opportunities which should be open to all staff and parents, as appropriate. The teacher evaluation system is another way to encourage critical thinking when administrators provide concrete observational feedback and reinforcement. New teacher mentor/mentee programs have proven quite effective for new teachers as well.

They receive guidance from the Board of Education and input from teachers, but ultimately, they have a crucial role to play in determining the direction of educational outcomes in their schools. To implement critical thinking as an integral part of the educational process, school administrators must not only agree that it is important but put in place guidelines to assist teachers to integrate it in all areas of the educational process.

BOARDS OF EDUCATION

Outside of teachers and administrators, boards of education can influence what is taught and how it is taught. Currently this is increasingly more challenging given pressure by citizens objecting to what is being taught.

Boards can have a positive impact by promoting guidelines for teaching critical thinking in the classroom. They can provide educational opportunities for teachers and encourage the purchase of critical-thinking materials for teachers and students. They can provide direction for school administrators to enhance critical-thinking opportunities for teachers and students. They can include parents, invite the community to meetings to present suggestions, and inform them about what the school district is doing to enhance critical-thinking skills. Many effective school systems include board members in their critical-thinking training events.

The school board is the top of the education pyramid in the community and should use its influence to promote critical thinking in and out of the classroom.

PARENTS

Parents may read the Hammes Classroom Experience and wonder how they can do this at home. Here are some general ways to integrate critical thinking into a child's everyday life. Relatively simple things parents can do to encourage basic critical thinking:

- Parents can model probative questions that children can adapt and utilize in their everyday activities and interactions.
- Initiate the habit of thinking critically. Ask children to critically evaluate music, food, video games, or other everyday topics and activities. Children are capable of evaluating pros and cons, value or lack of value, quality or lack of quality. For example, when an issue or action arises on a television show, pause it, and ask them what they think and why the issue as presented could be right or wrong. Or what is the value or lack of value. Or what could be done differently. How can this be utilized by them? This does not need to be sophisticated at first. Questions can be basic such as determining elementary differences or similarities.
- Parents can also engage their children in the art of debate. Ask what they like about something and then present another side and nudge them to prove this view wrong or theirs right. Best outcome is they can

be engaged to recognize the merits of both sides or multiple sides of a topic or issue.
- Make sure to have diverse reading materials available or offer them websites that contain quality points of view or information that will provide differing positions.
- Practice asking children to give evidence whenever they make a claim of some sort.
- Encourage children to do the same with the claims of others.
- Play games that require thinking that includes options or decision-making.
- Discuss with children why critical thinking is important for them by giving examples such as when friends want to do something, and the child is not sure it is the right thing to do. The goal is to provide the child with the skills to make the right choices.
- Ask questions to determine the ability of young children to solve problems. Instead of answering the child's questions directly, ask them clarifying questions such as *"What are your ideas?"* or *"How did you or can you solve the problem?"*
- Assist the child to learn how to guess in instances where they do not know the answer. This can encourage thinking creatively. It will help improve their skills in solving problems correctly.
- Teach the child to do research and look for more information. With technology advancements, the child will should be interested in browsing through the websites to find answers. The child should develop problem solving skills to think critically.
- Encourage children to consider advantages and disadvantages of taking actions or making decisions.

Most, if not all, of these actions can be started as soon as children develop expressive and receptive language skills and begin to offer their opinions and ask questions. Some of the *Obstacles to Clear Thinking* can be used in a modified form as well, using language appropriate for their age. Make a game of it. Present them with a situation occurring currently such as conflict about sharing a toy with a younger sibling? Why did the older sibling take the toy away? Could the sibling have done something differently or reacted differently? Basic questions cause children to think and analyze interactions. Initially parents may need to provide answers until the child can begin to understand how to analyze situations, ask questions, and offer options. This can be done with books children are reading as well. With the HCE materials, parents can begin to integrate many of the concepts by the time the child is five or six.

Parents can also utilize some of the recommendations provided in the section for elementary and middle school teachers. Build on the critical thinking children are learning in school. Or if the school is not using critical thinking regularly parents can still utilize various components of the HCE especially the *obstacles to clear thinking.*

To help encourage positive and healthy cognitive growth in a teen, parents can:

- Include them in discussions about a variety of topics, issues, and current events.
- Encourage the teen to share ideas and thoughts.
- Encourage teens to think independently and develop their ideas.
- Help them set goals.
- Challenge them to think about possibilities for the future.
- Compliment and praise the teen for well-thought-out decisions.[7]

It is better if schools are using critical thinking as a foundation for learning, but whether they are or not, parents can work with their children to be critical thinkers.

EMPLOYERS

Employers have been complaining for decades about how unprepared students leaving high school are for the work world. Often, they need to provide some additional classes to get new employees to a level wherein they can function effectively. This is especially of concern with problem solving and working with limited direction.

This can be an issue with college graduates as well. They may come prepared with knowledge in the field, but many have difficulty on the job if they are not given clear direction and are not monitored along the way. Whether high school or college graduates, employers are finding a large percentage of them unable to problem solve and analyze situations.

Although employers are hopeful the education system will provide more of these skills, it is incumbent on them to provide opportunities for employees to problem solve, offering them training on actual situations and having supervisors and managers engage employees in resolving problems.

Many of the techniques used in the HCE can be readily transferred to the workplace. If employers want to have workers that can do more than follow direction and accomplish what is expected, they need to provide opportunities to think critically and problem solve. College students and high school graduates bring a base of knowledge with them, but typically not extensive awareness of critical analysis, problem solving, and determining different ways to address tasks and issues. Using some of the obstacles to clear thinking provided, the group participation technique as well as brainstorming sessions that require all workers involved to actively participate will initiate the kind of thinking and expansion of ideas and solutions necessary for employers to grow their companies, remain competitive, and reduce turnover.

Employers should also engage more with educational institutions at various levels (high school, college, trade school, technical school, and others) in discussing their needs, the deficiencies they see in new employees, and how they can be directly or indirectly involved. They can form partnerships with them to ensure students are better prepared for the world of work. Using many of the same critical-thinking techniques provided in the classroom, employers can be active in developing these skills.

Below is a process developed by the Hammes Associates consulting firm that will engage employees, provide for analysis and critical thinking, and ultimately result in better decision-making and actions to attain improved outcomes.

The process is called FACTS:

Focus: What is the issue or action that needs a decision. How immediate is it? Determine a timeline for implementation or action.

Assess: What are the options available and what might reduce the effectiveness of each option and what the impact of each option should be.

Choose: After enumerating options, assessing their potential positives and negatives, choose the option that seems best.

Track: Determine how to monitor the process and determine effectiveness.

Shift: As the option unfolds what modifications are needed, what unforeseen things occurred.

If employers include a range of employees in the process to ensure a broad perspective of the issue or action, they will have engaged them in problem solving and critical thinking. Employees will be involved in offering a variety of options, analyzing their value and potential problems, determine which option seems best, and then doing ongoing monitoring and analysis. This involves employees in the business and gets them to be analytical and contribute beyond their day-to-day task completion. Do not choose only your best employees, because others may have ideas and may have capabilities that are untapped because they are never asked.

To encourage everyone to participate, use the group technique wherein everyone takes a few minutes to write down their thoughts on the issue or action. Then the leader asks each person to provide one of their ideas and they are written on a white board. Everyone had time to think and note their thoughts, so in this fashion even introverted employees will offer one idea. If you know who they are start with them, so they have an opportunity before the list of ideas is exhausted. Often if asked to spontaneously offer an idea, most will say they can't think of any, but if they have time to write down ideas, they will be more comfortable and share. If given an agenda beforehand, they can come prepared for the meeting and that is better. However, sometimes meetings are called spontaneously, or issues arise during a meeting that require input. If the latter occurs stop the discussion and ask everyone to write down the pros/cons, value/lack of value, or whatever assessment is needed. You want this discussion to occur during the meeting not afterward without you.

You can use this technique for each of the first three steps in the FACTS process as well, and again for the last step if changes need to be made. For each step use the technique and get the entire group involved.

Combined these two processes (FACTS and the group problem solving technique) will get employees to think about issues, offer suggestions, and discuss options. There are many people resources in companies that are never tapped. This will get them involved.

STUDENTS

With the information age explosion, students have access to a wealth of information. Not all of it is accurate or useful. In the HCE classroom, students feel empowered to ask for help sorting through information they read or hear. They are comfortable with small-group discussions to evaluate their opinions and the content they read and hear. They embrace critical thinking as an improved way to gain knowledge and insights. When encouraged, students question more and ask for alternative views or sources to expand their knowledge base.

However, as students, if critical thinking is not provided in the classroom, you could ask the teacher about varied methods to evaluate their learning and gently push against memorization focused tests (likely more in high school and beyond than earlier). It is understood that the author may be making this simpler than it is, but if there are a few students in every classroom seeking change, wanting varied activities, asking for different perspectives on an issue, questioning validity or exclusivity of information, many teachers will take notice.

Students can also speak with the administration or develop suggestions and submit them in written form. This is especially effective if there is a small group of students and ideas are presented in a manner that does not attack the current system but focuses on ideas to make it better for students and their education.

Hopefully, there will be students reading this book. If so, you can trumpet many of the suggestions provided in the HCE and elsewhere. Parents and teachers should promote these ideas and techniques, but students can also provide a powerful voice for change. The educational process impacts you the most, why not push for change that will make the experience more effective and valuable for you?

For the most part students feel powerless and just go with the flow. This book encourages you to have a voice.

This overview of what you can do, whatever your role, should serve to help you actively initiate critical thinking in the home, at school, at work, and in society. The tools, strategies, and techniques provided can be readily adapted and implemented. It takes the drive and desire to engage others in critical thinking and to make it the norm. Remember it is not just what you know, but how you came to know it, how you decided to accept it, and what you do with it.

NOTES

1. Quitadamo and Kurtz, "Learning to Improve," *Scientific American* (2007): 19–28.
2. Philip C. Abrami, Robert Bernard, Evgueni Borokhovski, Michael A. Surkes, Rana Tamim, and Dai Zhang, "Instructional Interventions Affecting Critical Thinking Skills," *Sage Journals 78*, no. 4 (2008): 31–39.
3. Atlasmission.com, 2022.
4. "Seven Ways to Teach Critical Thinking in Elementary School," Waldenu.edu.
5. Becton Loveless, "Critical Thinking Skills Guide," Education Corner, 2021, https://education corner.com/critical-thinking-skills.html..
6. Abrami et al., "Instructional Interventions."
7. Stanford Children's Health publication 2021.

Chapter 8

Hope for the Future

The greatest obstacle to those who hope to reform American education is complacency.

—Diane Ravitch

This quote sums up this book and the author's view on where we need to be headed in education in America. We cannot accept where it is because it has always been this way. We must actively pursue a better way, which from the author's perspective is incorporating critical thinking and analysis at every level of education.

During the Scopes trial which focused on teaching Darwin's theory of evolution in Tennessee public schools, Clarence Darrow made a significant point about hope. He was orating and making somewhat veiled sarcastic remarks about the court, rulings by the judge, and the process during the trial. The judge interrupted Darrow and said, "I hope you are not impugning the integrity of this court?" To which Darrow replied, "your honor has a right to hope."[1]

This is the state of education in this country. There is a right to hope it will move away from principally teaching content, a small array of facts, and tests that focus on memorization. That hope has not been very bright, but perhaps this book can be a part of the impetus for change.

Change can occur and is evidenced by the work of some teachers and school systems to provide some critical thinking exercises. But it is not enough, nor is there much impetus to change. Although the concern is at every level of education, it is critical in K–12 because these years lay the foundation for lifelong learning and the development of critical thinking skills. College teachers can implement it without students having prior awareness, but it is more difficult. It has been noted that the concerns continue into college wherein these teachers are also locked into the same educational process emphasizing memorization and teaching to the test. Throughout this book examples have been given of how school administrators and teachers are pressured by parents to raise and maintain the status of the school system. This means maintaining high academic ratings and having students' standardized test scores rank high in composite. It means ensuring that students get high grades so they can get into the college of their choice. Parents and businesses want high ranking schools because it reflects on the community and the value of property. They all perceive the best way to achieve this is with an educational system that focuses on agreed upon outcomes, which in most instances are high test scores and grades. "No misconception is so prevalent and so deceptive as the notion that liberal education is merely the communicating of factual information."[2] However, the overwhelming pressure to teach to the test is exactly this and impacts the potential that there is hope for a populace of critical thinkers and lifelong learners in the future.

There are issues that may block hope for changing the American classroom experience. Schools are regularly under attack for reasons that often have nothing to do with how to best educate children. In most cases, parents, teachers, and others in the community that have a vested interest in educational outcomes do not understand the need to focus on anything other than content memorization and grades. Parental and general community pressure to keep the educational process narrowly focused has been especially prevalent over the past few decades. Textbook developers are under pressure to limit what is published and the expectation is to keep books somewhat censored in the sense of not containing content that is viewed as controversial. "Textbooks that pile fact upon fact, while neglecting, especially in the human area, the problems to which conflicting ideas and values cluster, have dominated the scene. Education has not been notably successful as a liberating intellectual enterprise."[3] This is especially noteworthy because it was stated in the late 1960s and there is little evidence that things have changed. It may be even more constricting now.

Many think that education should follow the lead from the community. But what does the community know about education and how to produce the best citizens based on their education? Educators must lead and implement the educational system and processes that will best prepare students. Parents as stakeholders and other community members should be involved in a partnership with the school system to promote what is best for students. However, classroom instruction is not a community driven activity. Educators are trained for their profession and understand curriculum development, classroom management, learning strategies, and child development. They are certainly the "experts" to determine how to educate students.

The first line of action should come from teachers who have the credentials to engage with university departments of education and school administrators/boards of education to give more attention to critical thinking and analytical skills in the teacher training process. Currently college education departments do not emphasize critical thinking and logical analysis. Teachers graduating from college have been taught to develop their classroom based on use of a textbook and testing as a guide to outcomes and determination of their teaching abilities. Although this may be a difficult focus to change, this book provides tools, techniques, and ideas to implement critical thinking at all levels of education, in the home and in places of employment.

Teaching critical thinking begins with parents working with their children at an early age. Then as children enter school, parents and teachers working together as students advance from first to twelfth grade can ensure that critical thinking is a key part of the educational process. When parents and teachers do this, students are better prepared for further education, careers, and to be productive citizens.

Textbook publishers present their own challenges in presenting critical thinking in the classroom. Educators are relying on publishers and their sources to select the information they think students should know. There will be some bias in selecting material and this has been evident by who publishes these materials and where publishers are located. Most recently, individuals and groups appealing to textbook publishers to incorporate information related to the events associated with 1619, or Native Americans prior to and during European encroachment, and a realistic portrayal of the Civil War has been an uphill struggle. If trying to get new content into textbooks that more realistically reflects the early development of this country is a challenge, it is easy to assume it will be equally difficult to move the textbook industry to incorporate critical thinking and analysis. The fact that there is an uprising among many parents against teaching critical race theory (as well as by politicians and other power brokers) it will not be easy to push for another major shift in educational process via textbook additions and modifications. However, if publishers incorporated critical thinking and logical analysis throughout textbooks it might be easier to add factual but controversial material as well since there would be a format for critically analyzing content. Minimally, questions could be inserted that would cause teachers and students to evaluate the information presented.

There is some evidence of change in our educational institutions. For example, there is a growing movement to limit or eliminate the use of standardized test scores as a criterion for admission to college. Many schools of higher education are focusing more on essays, interviews, and other sources to determine viability for admission.

Another example of progress is utilization of the internet as a positive resource that expands the world, especially for younger children. It aids the expansion of visual and auditory content, which cannot be achieved in classrooms that only rely on a textbook. Rather than being overly concerned with internet content, parents, teachers, and others should give more attention to how to utilize it to broaden the knowledge base of children. Emphasizing digital comportment aids in helping students responsibly use the internet. Teachers should be of additional assistance to help students locate resources that are beneficial to their intellectual and emotional growth.

"The use of multi-sensory education could benefit all American students. Multi-sensory education gives students the skills to process information and develop strategies and critical thinking, rather than simply relying on memorization alone, which does not allow students to engage their brains, and apply the knowledge they are learning in the classroom to everyday situations and challenges."[4] In addition, a multi-sensory teaching approach allows learning access to students who learn differently.

Additionally, there is a growing movement toward self-directed learning, which points students in a direction and then encourages them to explore and use the teacher as a resource, sounding board, and filter.

The coming generation of teachers will have had their entire childhood in the age of the internet and the ever-growing access to information. They will be less content with textbook- only learning and engage students in a broader view of education and utilization of exploding information access.

Students will also push for change. They are wanting more use of alternative learning options, reduction or elimination of standardized tests, more preparation for everyday life, and more interactive classroom activities with the teacher and other students. Students may be the key agent that will change education.

> Since all education involves social, emotional, and academic learning, we have but two choices: We can either ignore that fact and accept disappointing results or address these needs. The promotion of social, emotional, and academic learning is not a shifting educational fad; it is the substance of education itself. It is not a distraction from the "real work" of math, English, or any other instruction; it is how instruction can succeed. And it is not another reason for political polarization. It brings together a traditionally conservative emphasis on local control and on the character of all students, and a historically progressive emphasis on the creative and challenging art of teaching and the social and emotional needs of all students, especially those who have experienced the greatest challenges.[5]

Although there remain many concerns with the current state of education, there is hope for the movement of education away from memorization and standardized tests as the benchmark of quality education. Of course, introducing some or all of the techniques noted in the Hammes Classroom Experience would move the process along much more quickly. The hope is that teachers, administrators, students, parents, employers, and the community at large will push the educational monolith toward more rapid expansion of critical thinking and maximize its potential.

FINAL QUOTES

Here are some quotes from a range of thinkers to put the end point on this book.

> The essence of the independent mind lies not in what it thinks, but in how it thinks.—Christopher Hitchins, *Letters to a Young Contrarian*, 2020
>
> Your education is one thing they cannot take away from you.—Elin Nordegren, MeMatra Education, 2022
>
> One of the problems with today's intelligentsia (and this occurs in every time period) is they have amnesia in the sense that they think they are doing original work, when much of what they tout was done decades or centuries ago, but unremembered or ignored. —Richard Hammes, paraphrasing an unremembered writer from the late twentieth century
>
> If you do not believe that knowledge for its own sake is a valid goal, then you are in the wrong place and if you do not insist on knowing then you are definitely in the wrong place.—Henry Ottinger, "Why the Class Failed," *New York Times*, July 22, 1971
>
> Where you stand depends upon where you sit.—Rufus Miles, September 1978, "The Origin and Meaning of Miles' Law," *Public Administration Review*

This seemingly simple final quote reflects the essence of this book, because what you say and believe is related to the educational biases you received, what your job/career is, the people that influenced you, where you reside, what you defend as the facts, and more. In sum, we must all think critically to overcome our biases based on where we and everyone else sits.

NOTES

1. Irving Stone, *Clarence Darrow for the Defense* (Kolkata, India: Signet, 1971), 147.
2. Arthur Bestor, *Educational Wastelands* (Champaign: University of Illinois Press, 1953), 96.

3. H. Gordon Hullfish and Philip G. Smith, *Reflective Thinking: The Method of Education* (New York: Dodd, Mead & Co., 1968), 147.

4. Ben Shifrin, head of a private school in Maryland, "Instead of Memorizing Facts, Our Kids Need Real Education," *Baltimore Sun*, February 1, 2021.

5. A Nation at Hope, howlearninghappens@americaspromise.org, October 2018.

Bibliography

Abrami, Philip C., Robert Bernard, and Eygueni Borokhovski. "How Does Distance Education Compare with Classroom Instruction? A Meta-Analysis of the Empirical Literature." *American Educator* (Fall 2004): 379–439.

Abrami, Philip, Robert Bernard, Evgueni Borokhovski, Michael A. Surkes, Rana Tamim, and Dai Zhang. "Instructional Interventions Affecting Critical Thinking Skills." *Sage Journals* 78, no. 4 (2008): 31–39.

Arum, Richard, and Josipa Roksa. *Academically Adrift*. Chicago: University of Chicago Press, 2011.

Atlasmission.com, 2022.

Barzun, Jacques. *The House of Intellect*. New York: Harper Perennial, 2002.

Bestor, Arthur. *Educational Wastelands*. Champaign: University of Illinois Press, 1953.

Bloom, Benjamin. *Taxonomy of Educational Objectives: The Classification of Educational Goals*. Harlow, UK: Longman, 1971.

———. Bloomstaxonomy.net.

Bransford, John. "Teaching Thinking and Problem Solving: Research Foundations." *American Psychologist* 41, no. 10 (1986): 1078–89.

Butler, Heather A., Christopher Pentoney, and Mabelle P. Bong. "Predicting Real-World Outcomes." *Thinking Skills and Creativity* 25 (2017): 38–46.

The Center for Critical Thinking. criticalthinking.org.

DeSilver, Drew. "U.S. Students' Academic Achievement Still Lags That of Their Peers in Many Other Countries." Pew Research Center, February 2019. https://www.pewresearch.org/fact-tank/2017/02/15/u-s-students-internationally-math-science/.

Dewey, John. *The Later Works of John Dewey, 1949–1952*, vol. 16. Carbondale: Southern Illinois University Press, 2008.

Elder, Linda. criticalthinking.org.

Ellerton, Peter. Creative Commons, January 2020. https://creativecommons.org/2019/12/09/save-the-date-public-domain-day-2020-is-happening-in-january-in-washington-d-c/.

Farber, Jerry. *The Student as N . . . er*. Los Angeles: Los Angeles Free Press, 1967.

Farnsworth, Ward. *The Socratic Method: A Practitioner's Handbook*. Boston: David Godine, 2021.

Gardner, Howard. *The Disciplined Mind: The Education Every Child Deserves*. New York: Penguin, 1999.

Hart Research Associates. "It Takes More than a Major: Employer Priorities for College Learning and Student Success," (April 2013) 1–15.

Henderson, Charles, and Melissa H. Dancy. "Barriers to the Use of Research-Based Instructional Strategies: The Influence of Both Individual and Situational Characteristics." *Physical Review Physics Education Research* 3, no. 2 (2007): 020102-1–020102-14.

Hook, Sidney. *Education for the Modern*. New York: Dial Press, 1946.

hooks, bell. *Teaching to Transgress: Education as the Practice of Freedom*. New York: Routledge, 1994.

Hullfish, H. Gordon, and Philip G. Smith. *Reflective Thinking: The Method of Education*. New York: Dodd, Mead and Co., 1968.

Hutchins, Robert. *The Conflict in Education in a Democratic Society*. New York: Harper and Bros., 1956.

———. "The Idea of a College." *Center Magazine* 5, no. 3 (1972): 45–49. Reprinted from *Measure* 1 (Fall 1950): 363–71.

———. *No Friendly Voice*. Chicago: University of Chicago Press, 1936.

———. *The University Utopia*. Chicago: University of Chicago Press, 1953.

Jaschik, Scott. "Well Prepared in Their Own Eyes." insidehighered.com, January 2015.

Kramer, Lindsay. "What are the Benefits of Critical Thinking in the Workplace?" *Houston Chronicle*, July 2020.

Lesgold, Alan. "The Nature and Methods of Learning and Doing." *The American Psychologist* (November 2001): 24–33.

Library of Congress. Education Study, 1984, https://eric.ed.gov/?id=ED261706.

Loveless, Becton. "Critical Thinking Skills Guide." Education Corner, 2021. https://educationcorner.com/critical-thinking-skills.html.

McGranahan, Lucas. "Defining Figure." *The University of Chicago Magazine*, Spring 2021.

Minnow, Newton H. Chairman Federal Communications Commission, speech. https://time.com/4315217/newton-minow-vast-wasteland-1961-speech.

A Nation at Hope. howlearninghappens@americaspromise.org.

Nisbett, Richard. *The Geography of Thought*. Glencoe, IL: Free Press, 2003.

Ottinger, Henry. "Why the Class Failed." *New York Times*, July 22, 1971.

Peeples, Shanna. *Think Like Socrates*. Thousand Oaks, CA: Corwin, 2019.

Perkins, David. *Future Wise: Educating Our Children for a Changing World*. San Francisco: Josey-Bass, 2014.

Plato. *Early Socratic Dialogues*. Edited by Trevor J. Saunders. London: Penguin Classics, 2005.

Plaut, Suzanne. *The Right to Literacy in Secondary Schools: Creating a Culture of Thinking*. New York: Teachers College Press, 2012.

Preciado, Paul. *An Apartment in Uranus*. Los Angeles: Semiotext(e), 2019.

Principles of Mathematics and Logic: A Course for Liberal Arts Students. R.A.G. Seely Mathematics Department, John Abbott College, Ste Anne de Bellevue, QC 2020.

Quitadamo, J., and Kurtz, M. "Learning to Improve." *Scientific American* (2007): 19–28.

Rauch, Jonathan. *The Constitution of Knowledge: A Defense of Truth*. Washington, DC: Brookings Institution Press, 2021.

Sawyer and others. unl.edu/gradstudies/socratic-questioning 2000.

Siefer, Linda. "Assessing General Education Learning Outcomes." *Peer Review* (Fall/Winter 2011): 9–12. https://www.nyu.edu/content/dam/nyu/academicAssessment/documents/2014AcademicAssessmentSymposium/Peer%20Review_Vol%2013(4)_Assessing%20Liberal%20Education%20Outcomes%20Using%20VALUE%20Rubrics.pdf.

Shifrin, Ben. "Instead of Memorizing Facts, Our Kids Need Real Education." *Baltimore Sun*, February 1, 2021.

Sizer, Theodore. *Horace's Hope: What Works for the American High School*. Boston: Mariner Books, 1997.

———. *Redesigning the American High School*. Boston: Houghton Mifflin, 1992.

Stanford Children's Health. Cognitive Development in the Teen Years. https://www.stanfordchildrens.org/en/topic/default?id=cognitive-development-in-adolescence-90-P01594.

Stone, Irving. *Clarence Darrow for the Defense*. Kolkata, India: Signet, 1971.

Tatsumi, Ana. "Teaching Critical Thinking in the Language Classroom." *World of Better Learning* (blog), April 4, 2018. https://www.cambridge.org/elt/blog/2018/04/04/teaching-critical-thinking/.

Toffler, Alvin. *Future Shock*. New York: Penguin Random House, 1970.

Van Gelder, Tim. "Teaching Critical Thinking." *College Teaching* (Winter 2005): 41–48.

Whitehead, Alfred North. *Science and the Modern World*. New York: Simon and Schuster, 1997.

Willingham, Daniel. *The Reading Mind*. Hoboken, NJ: Jossey-Bass, 2017.

Woodhouse, Howard. "The Concept of Growth in Bertrand Russell's Educational Thought." *Journal of Educational Thought* 17, no. 1 (1983): 12–22.

Zulfiqar, Anisa. "The Importance of Teaching Critical Thinking to Students." *Pearson Partnership* (blog), June 30, 2018. https://www.talentlens.com.au/blog/teaching-critical-thinking-to-students.

About the Author

Dr. Richard Hammes was president of Hammes Associates, a management and human resource consulting firm located in metropolitan Chicago, Illinois, with a national presence. He continues to do some occasional consulting work with long-term client companies.

The impetus for this book is his college and graduate school experiences as well as his teaching of introductory and other psychology courses at several Chicago area community colleges for more than forty years. Additionally, Dr. Hammes' doctorate focused on learning and developmental psychology provides an academic credential. His consulting work provides a unique opportunity to bring his academic knowledge into the work world and helped grow his consulting business with learning and development materials in the work world. He has a unique blending of academia and business and industry.

Dr. Hammes, is an organizational psychologist with extensive experience in management and human resource consulting. Prior to transitioning to corporate consulting in the early 1980s, Dr. Hammes was a clinician and manager for thirteen years in the public and private sectors of the mental health care industry.

Dr. Hammes has more than thirty years of experience providing objective assessments for candidate selection and promotion, succession planning and career development, leadership/management coaching and consulting, performance management, personal development, meetings management, outplacement, career development, and other management and human resource services and programs. Based on his years as a consultant (individual consulting and group workshops), he has written training manuals on (1) career development, (2) job search, (3) management skills, (4) leadership skills, (5) effective communication, (6) team functioning, (7) performance appraisal/management, (8) meetings management, and (9) manager interview training.

Dr. Hammes is a member of the American Psychological Association. He has an undergraduate degree from the University of Wisconsin and graduate degrees from the University of Chicago and Northern Illinois University, with a doctorate focused on Learning and Developmental Psychology. He is the author of numerous articles on management, leadership, and employee development.

www.ingramcontent.com/pod-product-compliance
Lightning Source LLC
Chambersburg PA
CBHW030144240426
43672CB00005B/264